THE STORY OF EXPLORATION

EXPLORING
CAVES

ABDO
Publishing Company

THE STORY OF EXPLORATION

EXPLORING
CAVES

BY REBECCA FELIX

CONTENT CONSULTANT
JASON POLK
ASSISTANT PROFESSOR OF GEOSCIENCE
WESTERN KENTUCKY UNIVERSITY

CREDITS

Published by ABDO Publishing Company, PO Box 398166, Minneapolis, MN 55439. Copyright © 2014 by Abdo Consulting Group, Inc. International copyrights reserved in all countries. No part of this book may be reproduced in any form without written permission from the publisher. The Essential Library™ is a trademark and logo of ABDO Publishing Company.

Printed in the United States of America,
North Mankato, Minnesota
102013
012014

Editor: Arnold Ringstad
Series Designer: Emily Love

Photo credits: Galyna Andrushko/Shutterstock Images, cover, 2–3; Vitalii Nesterchuk/Shutterstock Images, 6–7; Doug Meek/Shutterstock Images, 8–9; Petr Vostrovsky/Shutterstock Images, 14–15; Seth Resnick/Science Faction/SuperStock, 16–17; Hung Chung Chih/Shutterstock Images, 20–21; Exactostock/SuperStock, 23, 50–51, 58–59; National Park Service, 26–27, 44, 47; hangingpixels/Shutterstock Images, 28–29; Patrick Rolands/Shutterstock Images, 31; iStockphoto/Thinkstock, 32–33, 125; LatitudeStock/SuperStock, 34–35; imagebroker.net/SuperStock, 38–39; Wikimedia Commons, 53; Red Line Editorial, 55, 60, 132; age fotostock/SuperStock, 56–57, 133 (bottom left); Stephen L. Alvarez/National Geographic Creative, 64, 104, 115, 118–119, 133 (top left); Robbie Shone/Aurora Open/SuperStock, 66–67; Nick Hewetson/DK Images, 70–71; Jenni Vincen/Journal Newspaper/AP Images, 74; Bern Szukalski/AP Images, 79; Dray van Beeck/Shutterstock Images, 80–81; J. Ganter/National Geographic Creative, 82; Prisma/SuperStock, 85, 133 (bottom right); Tips Images/SuperStock, 88–89; Design Pics/Thinkstock, 92–93; Arctic-Images/SuperStock, 94–95; Stock Connection/SuperStock, 97; Hazel Barton, 99, 133 (top right); Matt Jeppson/Shutterstock Images, 101; Subbotina Anna/Shutterstock Images, 106–107; Tom Grundy/Shutterstock Images, 108–109; Michael Runkel/SuperStock, 111; salsjean/Shutterstock Images, 122–123; Carsten Peter/Speloresearch & Films/National Geographic Creative, 127; Shutterstock Images, 132

Library of Congress Control Number: 2013946594
Cataloging-in-Publication Data

Felix, Rebecca, 1984-
 Exploring caves / Rebecca Felix.
   p. cm. -- (The story of exploration)
 Includes bibliographical references and index.
 ISBN 978-1-62403-249-3
 1. Caves--Juvenile literature. 2. Cave ecology--Juvenile literature. 3. Caves--Discovery and exploration--Juvenile literature.
 I. Title.
 551.44--dc23

                                        2013946594

CONTENTS

Cave explorers must use special equipment to stay safe while investigating the steep drops, slippery rocks, and hidden crevices of Earth's largest caves.

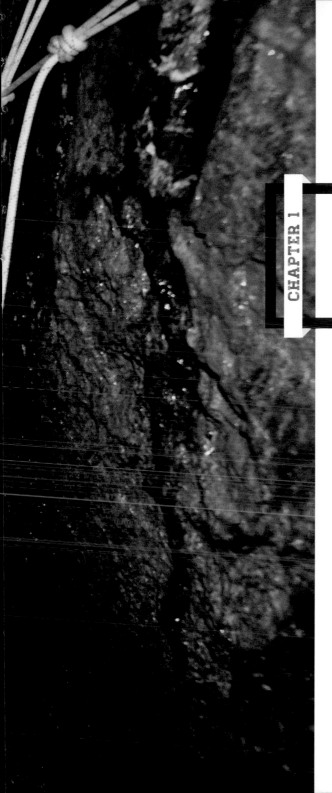

CHAPTER 1

THE EIGHTH CONTINENT

Descending into darkness, three pairs of feet hit hard stone with relief. The threat of poisonous snakes waiting to strike from the inky black depths was gone, at least for the moment. A narrow flooded tunnel allowed just enough space for the explorers to slither through, hands and knees pushing forward through rushing water. The tunnel ended suddenly as the water dropped into a void below.

One of the explorers used ropes to lower herself down the hole. As she followed the water's path, her headlamp lit up the cascades of water pushing her down toward the darkness. The others met her at the bottom. They came to a rocky tunnel filled with water. Attempting to climb through the tunnel underwater was no use. It was too tight a squeeze.

The explorers were at a dead end, deep in the darkness, hundreds of feet below Earth's surface. There was no way out but to retrace their steps, this time going up.

Cavers Jim Brown, Andrea Hunter, and Bill Stone were in the Aguacate River Sink Cave, deep in the forest of Oaxaca, Mexico. Finding pitch-black tunnels, underground

DANGER IN THE DARK

Many cave passages are hundreds or thousands of feet below the surface. That far underground, the darkness is total. This makes every movement dangerous, especially in unpredictable cave environments where giant formations, steep holes, drop-offs, and huge hunks of falling rock are common. To navigate caves, explorers rely on artificial lights such as headlamps and flashlights. Light is so essential to their safety it is rationed. Cavers try to use lights only when actively exploring, meaning resting and eating are often done in complete darkness. Cavers who spend too much time in the dark can start to hallucinate, hearing and seeing things that are not really there.

Once caves have been explored and mapped, these strange, alien-looking areas sometimes become attractions for tourists.

waterfalls, and crushingly tight rock passages were common occurrences. It was March 2004, and they were on the fourth week of a grueling nine-week underground expedition. It was just one part of Stone's years-long quest to discover the deepest cave on Earth. He was not alone in his search. Cavers explore for many reasons: to break records, make geologic discoveries, unearth archaeological artifacts, or study unique cave habitats and organisms. Many have a goal to push caves, which means going beyond what is known and explored. Some caving teams spend days on end without a glimpse of sunlight, exploring otherworldly underground terrain. They push through miles of tunnels, mazes of boulders the size of trucks, and into gaping holes with no end in sight. They dive beneath pitch-black underground lakes and scramble down waterfalls. They sleep on stone and wake to do it all again—or climb back to the surface when they reach a dead end.

THE LAST FRONTIER

The world below Earth's surface is a realm of twisted tunnels, colossal caverns, underground waterfalls, and never-ending darkness. Crystals, towering rocks, creatures without eyes, and globs of unique microbes are common in caves. But even features common above the surface become otherworldly deep underground, which is why this subterranean world is sometimes called the "eighth continent."[1] It is one of the last frontiers on Earth that can be explored only by humans. Scientists are developing robots and probes that can help, but humans are still the most effective cave explorers.

By the 2000s, man was looking for something new to explore. Man had walked on the moon and discovered the South and North Poles. People had successfully scaled the world's highest mountain, Mount Everest, in Tibet. And they had dived to the deepest-known point in the world's oceans, a

GRUELING EXPLORATION

Cave exploration can be difficult work. One author describes caving in harsh terms:

> [Caving is] weeks of rappelling down and climbing up immense vertical drops with huge loads, banging like human wrecking balls into rock faces, scraping through rib-cracking squeezes, destroying knees on steep breakdown piles, worming through spine-twisting breakdown, all the while soaked and verging on hypothermia, buried in perpetual darkness, malnourished, [and] sleep-deprived.[2]

valley called Challenger Deep in the Mariana Trench of the Pacific Ocean. But the deepest cave on Earth remained a mystery. Although there are current records for the deepest point reached within a cave, the absolute deepest cave on Earth cannot be confirmed until humans or robots reach the bottoms of each cave worldwide. This discovery will be a key benchmark in humankind's search to discover the secret frontiers of the world. Deep cave expeditions are undertaken each year. But even when new depth records are not set, there are also many smaller discoveries: new passages, species, or artifacts.

Cave exploration provides valuable insights and contributions to the scientific fields of archaeology, geology,

REMOTE CAVE EXPLORATION

Technology has advanced greatly in many fields of exploration in recent years. Robots and probes scout other planets and moons. Mechanical devices traverse human intestines and document their surroundings with video footage. Because cave exploration can be difficult and dangerous, some question why it is not done remotely by camera or robot technology. Although this technology may become available, it will not replace human exploration. Investigating caves requires a level of awareness, real-time reasoning, and environment and situation processing technology cannot yet match. Combined with the human desire to explore, this means people will remain the primary explorers of caves for years to come.

and mineralogy. It can also help scientists learn how Earth formed, uncover oil reserves, and protect underground reservoirs of drinking water. Caving is grueling, challenging, thrilling work. However, many have seen it as less glamorous than other kinds of exploration. Polar and space exploration have been much more popular among the general public. This in part is due to a cave's makeup. It is impossible to see a complete cave system unless looking at a drawn map. Because caves can consist of a huge network of darkened tunnels and caverns, it was difficult to take good cave photos for many years.

Though they are among the oldest features of our planet, caves have remained largely mysterious. People are making new, surprising discoveries all the time. Explorers have found cave chambers large enough to enter by free-fall skydive, crystals the size of tree trunks, underwater caverns, and tiny creatures that come back to life after being frozen solid. Technology to document these discoveries has evolved, allowing even noncavers a glimpse into the amazing worlds thriving beneath their feet. This

Underwater caves are among the most fascinating areas on Earth, but they are also the most dangerous caves to explore.

new dimension of documentation illuminates the dark wonders of caves and the intense passion of those who explore them.

Glacier caves can change shape much more quickly than those formed in stone.

CHAPTER 2

CAVE FORMATION AND FEATURES

Caves are naturally formed voids large enough to accommodate human exploration. There are many types of caves, and they form in several ways. Most caves occur in stone. Glacier caves, however, form in the ice of a glacier. As the glacier shifts and moves, cracks form. Melting ice from the glacier's surface drains down into small glacier cracks and carves a shaft.

Caves in stone are larger, more common, and more permanent than those in glaciers. There are several different types of stone caves. Talus caves occur between mountainside boulder piles. Volcanic caves develop from lava in volcanic rock. When a volcano erupts, lava spills down its sides like a stream. The hot material cuts a small bed down the side of the volcano. The sides, floor, and surface of the lava stream harden, creating a lava tube. As the hot lava in the center flows downward, it leaves a hollow passage of hardened lava rock behind called a volcanic cave.

Wind and water can also physically erode stone to create caves. Wind wears away small caverns called eolian caves, which are often found in desert sandstone cliffs. Sandstone is one example of a stronger rock, which, when layered in bedrock near a weaker rock, such as shale, creates a type of cave called a rock shelter. Elements wear away the exposed areas of the weaker

GETTING SMALLER AND SMALLER: GLACIER CAVES

The passages of limestone caves grow larger over time, as groundwater dissolves away stone. Glacier caves behave differently. Although meltwater initially forms glacier caves, the walls of a passage eventually squeeze shut. This is due to the massive weight and pressure of the surrounding glacier ice. Chambers and passages squeeze into tight cracks, making entrances that once accommodated humans impassible or even invisible over time.

rock, and the stronger rock remains intact, becoming exposed as the cave's roof and walls.

Sea caves are coastal openings in cliffs or beaches. They are created when waves continually batter rock in one place, slowly carving an opening. Water also wears away certain types of stone through chemical reactions to form solution caves. Of all cave types, solution caves are the most common. They are also among the largest in the world.

SOLUTION CAVES

Most solution caves form in a type of terrain known as karst. This landscape consists of soluble rocks: limestone, dolomite, and gypsum. These soluble rocks were once chemical deposits on the ancient seafloor. When the sea level falls, the karst terrain is exposed. In other cases, the rocks are pushed upward by Earth's natural forces over millions of years, becoming karst terrain. Within karst rock layers are small cracks where water, mostly from precipitation or melting snow, can enter after passing through the soil. The water mixes with carbon dioxide in the

Karst landscapes often feature dramatic erosion, whether below the ground or above it.

air and soil and becomes slightly acidic, creating carbonic acid. The carbonic acid dissolves calcium carbonate, the main mineral in the soluble rock of karst landscapes. This process forms caves over the course of hundreds, thousands, or even millions of years.

In rare instances, other types of acids, such as sulfuric acid, carve solution caves. This occurs when the acids rise from deep inside Earth and react with oxygen in the air, forming an acidic solution that carves caves from the bottom up.

KARST

Karst landscapes are found across the globe, making up approximately 15 percent of Earth's land surface.[1] The Yucatán Peninsula in South America as well as parts of France, England, Ireland, and China have karst landscapes. In the United States, high concentrations of karst are found in several states, including Kentucky, Tennessee, and Florida, with smaller clusters of karst found in nearly all corners of the country. Karst topography varies from low, rocky plains and elevated stone plateaus to huge cone and tower formations. The high and narrow tower karst in southern China is especially visually stunning, with some towers reaching more than 650 feet (200 m) high.[2]

SOLUTION CAVE LIFE CYCLES

Over the course of thousands or millions of years, groundwater eats away at fractures in soluble rock in a series of solution cave life stages. Limestone caves usually have a life span of several million years.

The first stage of a solution cave is called the inception stage. This stage begins with tiny fractures in bedrock. During this stage, which may last as long as 10,000 years, these fractures widen.[3] As the calcite is slowly worn away below, other features develop, such as sinkholes, springs, aquifers, and sinking streams. Sinkholes and sinking streams feed water to the caves, increasing the flow of water upon completion of this stage. This causes the limestone to dissolve more quickly, leading to the enlargement stage.

The enlargement stage can last from 10,000 to millions of years. During this time, groundwater carves small pockets into passages, which can eventually grow hundreds of feet wide or tall. When cave passages stop enlarging and are at least partially filled with air, they are in a stage of stagnation. Passages large enough to allow

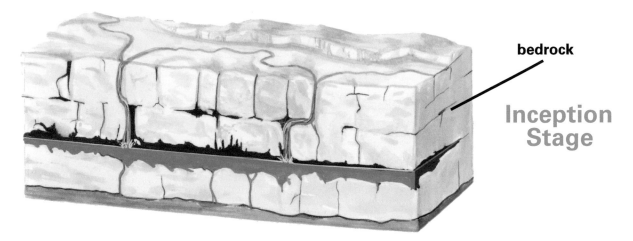

bedrock

Inception Stage

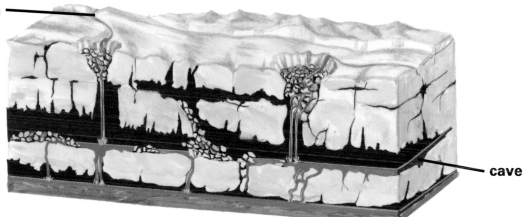

sinking stream

Enlargement Stage

cave

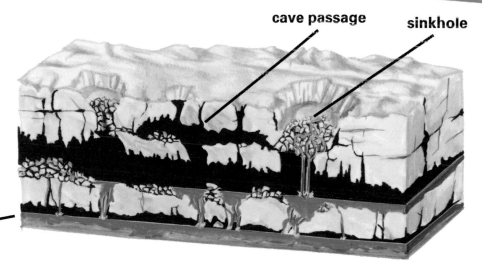

cave passage

sinkhole

Stagnation Stage

aquifer

human exploration are considered caves. When several cave passages connect, they form a cave system. It is during the period of stagnation most people explore caves and their fascinating formations. Few changes occur inside the cave during this stage, though surface erosion continues to alter the above landscape.

CAVE FEATURES

Cave passages vary greatly in size and shape, from narrow cracks to huge chambers. Caves can be dusty and dry, but most are damp and contain streams, lakes, and waterfalls. The way water flowed through during formation is the greatest influence on passage shape. Passages formed while fully flooded are shaped somewhat like tubes. This is because erosion occurred in every direction roughly equally. If air flowed above the surface of the water, less erosion affected

DIRECTIONAL WATER POWER

The direction water flows as it erodes cave walls plays a large role in determining the size of an opening. Vertically flowing water can carve out huge pitches, eroding more rock as it plunges. Horizontally flowing water is often slower, but it can contact the rock for longer periods and over greater distances. This ultimately gives horizontal water more dissolving power. The largest cave passages in the world are horizontal.

the upper part of the cave. This results in a passage much deeper than it is wide. Cave passages can also be twisting, tight, and narrow. The structure of bedrock as well as speed and volume of flowing water also influence passage shape.

Horizontal passages are most common in solution caves. These passages are often shaped somewhat similar to steep stairs, with a vertical pitch dropping to short stretches of horizontal passageways called meanders. Pitches and meanders can descend vertically or branch off horizontally, depending on the cave system. Pitches can be dry, or they might hold cascading waterfalls leading to water-filled pits. Completely flooded passages are called sumps. Under a sump's surface, the passage may end, similar to the bottom of a lake, or it may continue, leading into other passages or chambers.

Some cave passages are formed by collapse. Ceilings will cave in, enlarging a passage into a large open cavity, which is known as a chamber. Other collapses block passages with what are called breakdowns.

Flowing water in caves often creates large horizontal passages.

CAVE FORMATIONS

The walls of a cave can be smooth from water erosion or decorated with structural textures or elements. Speleothems are mineral cave features formed by calcite deposits, sometimes over thousands or even millions of years. The groundwater solution that forms caves contains amounts of the calcite it dissolves from the stone. When the cavern grows large enough to accommodate air along with the water that has formed it, the air absorbs some of the water's carbon dioxide. The reduction in carbon dioxide reduces the water's ability to hold the calcite it dissolved from the rock, and so the calcite is redeposited. There are several types of speleothems. Stalactites are formations emerging from cave ceilings and walls. Stalagmites are formations of mineral deposits that collect on cave floors when water drips from above.

Stalactites form when a rock fracture in a cave drips water. When the drop of water hits the air, it falls toward the floor, but it leaves behind a small ring of calcium carbonate on the ceiling or wall surface. As each drip forms and falls, another ring is left behind. The stalactite forms with a hollow inner canal that allows each drip to reach the end of the formation and build upon the last ring. Eventually, these rings take on a variety of shapes, from long, spindly tubes that resemble icicles to great sweeping sheets that resemble drapery, called flowstone.

In passages with dry floors, the drops from a stalactite hit the floor, creating stalagmites. Some are fragile spindles reaching toward their stalactite creators. Others grow wide and domelike. Because stalagmites do not have a hollow canal within, as their stalactite counterparts do, they can grow very large without breaking. Stalactites, on the other hand, may

Stalactites, stalagmites, and columns are among the most famous cave formations.

fall and shatter if they grow too large. Sometimes a long stalactite and tall stalagmite meet, creating a formation called a column.

Drier caves often have formations of crystals, created when water evaporates and mineral deposits are left behind. They are ideal environments for slow-growing crystals. Because their underground location protects them from most weather conditions, most caves retain a somewhat constant temperature and humidity level. The outside environment influences temperature, but in a more steady way. Most caves have a temperature that is the long-term average of temperatures that occur above them.

Cave formations can occur within all parts of a cave. These parts are often described as zones. The entrance zone is the area immediately following a cave entrance or opening. The twilight zone is the middle zone where caves get darker, but some light from the surface still reaches the area. The deep cave zone is the deepest zone and the most detached from the surface. In this area there is no natural light at all.

Cave entrances are sometimes well hidden by natural features.

To explore these zones, cavers must first find a cave's entrance on the surface. But not all caves have visible surface entrances, meaning cavers must have an understanding of where to begin the hunt for access. To find these openings, humans have developed skills and gained knowledge about caves through years of interaction dating back to the dawn of civilization.

Cave paintings and other artifacts provide vivid evidence of the lives of people who lived in prehistoric cultures.

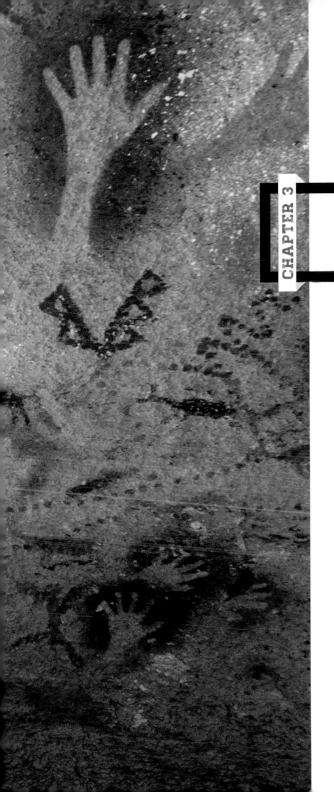

CHAPTER 3

CAVING HISTORY

Tucked away from the elements, and with near-constant temperature and humidity, caves are a safe haven and rich resource for remnants of ancient civilizations. Among the oldest archaeological cave finds are a human finger and jawbone believed to be 1.2 million years old discovered in Elephant Chasm in Atapuerca, Spain, in 2007. Six years later, in 2013, a carved flint estimated to be 1.4 million years old was discovered in the same cave.[1]

Hundreds of thousands of years ago, caves were home to ancient people. The Neanderthal, sometimes known in popular culture as cavemen, appeared during prehistoric times, between 100,000 and 300,000 years ago. Neanderthals lived alongside anatomically modern humans, but they eventually vanished from the fossil record between 35,000 to 24,000 years ago.[2]

CAVE ARCHAEOLOGY

Caves are considered prime archaeological sites, as artifacts found within them are usually in the same spot ancient persons left them. These artifacts offer many clues about the way ancient cultures lived. Researchers have discovered art, skeletons, mummified bodies, and artifacts such as tools within the caves in Europe, Asia, and the Americas used for shelter by prehistoric cultures. Artifacts also suggest these people used caves for rituals, ceremonies, and burials.

People have discovered many works of art in the form of paintings or engravings on cave walls. There exists debate about whether Neanderthals

Caves once served as shelters and places of worship for prehistoric people, making them treasure troves for artifacts.

were advanced enough to create these works or if modern humans from that time produced them. The oldest of these works is believed to be located in El Castillo Cave in Spain, estimated to be 40,800 years old.[3] The walls of Chauvet Cave in France hold artwork created approximately 35,000 years ago, and Lascaux, France, is home to caves containing art that is approximately 20,000 years old.[4] Altamira Cave in Spain and the famous Cueva de las Manos in Argentina are among the many other locales with ancient art on cave walls.

Ancient literature was also preserved in caves. Beginning in 1947, Hebrew scrolls dating back to the 200s BCE were found in 11

CAVE ART

The ancient artwork discovered on cave walls sparks intrigue and endless study. The artwork in many caves was mainly created with paints made from minerals. Depictions of ancient horses, bison, lions, and even rhinoceroses line the walls of Chauvet Cave, and researchers have deemed them advanced for their estimated 35,000-year-old age.[5] Altamira Cave holds famous paintings and engravings. Among the depictions are various animals, as well as handprints. The cave most famous for its handprint art is Cueva de las Manos, or Cave of the Hands. The extensive art in this cave has been particularly well studied and consists of artistically grouped outlines of human hands, in addition to animals. The art dates as far back as 13,000 years ago.[6] Ancient South American civilizations created layers for the paintings, adding and extending the artwork in this cave.

sea caves overlooking the Dead Sea in the West Bank region of Palestine. The more than 800 scrolls consist of biblical texts that have influenced historians' beliefs about early religious history.[7] The scrolls are collectively considered one of the greatest archaeological finds of all time.

In addition to artifacts, art, and literature, people have also discovered archaic human remains in caves. In 2013, researchers unearthed 3,000-year-old bodies of 66 people in Harimaru, or Tiger Cave, in Sumatra, Indonesia. The number of bodies astounded the archaeologists. Previous discoveries included rock art, animal remains, and tools of the ancient Indonesian farmers who inhabited the cave. In Cueva de la Candelaria in Coahuila, Mexico, researchers discovered a mummified dog estimated to be 1,000 years old. It is one of the few mummified animals ever discovered in the world.

MAYA

Ruins in the Yucatán Peninsula in Central America revealed an ancient civilization dependent on caves. Historians

Sacred water-filled sinkholes were key features of Mayan cities.

estimate the Maya emerged in 1500 BCE. They lived in structures made of great stone blocks carved from the limestone, the rock making up the majority of the peninsula's landscape. The karst landscape of the region contains many caves and sinkholes.

The Maya built their cities around these karst features. Nearly all surface ruins of significant structures are located directly above natural or manmade wells. In the northern and central parts of the peninsula, there are no lakes or rivers above the surface. Climbing into caves to access freshwater in deep underground reservoirs was critical to survival for the Maya. The Maya also believed caves were the dwelling places of gods and deities, and they performed many rituals and sacrifices underground.

To reach cave depths, the Maya used cables and ladders made of vines. In the 1830s and 1840s, centuries after the Spanish conquered the Maya in the 1500s, explorers entered the caves. They found artifacts giving them insight into the ancient Mayan way of life. Researchers determined Belize's Actun Tunichil Muknal, or Cave of the Crystal Sepulchre, was a sacrificial site. There, archaeologists discovered remains of a woman they believe was sacrificed for religious purposes, as well as burial remains of 14 other Mayans. The cave also contains broken pottery and two monuments used to collect the blood of elite Mayans after they cut themselves with sharp obsidian rocks as an offering to their gods.

Both dry and underwater Mayan caves across the peninsula proved to hold similar archaeological treasures. These include human remains thought

CITIES OF RUIN

The ruins of great Mayan cities, temples, and caves have intrigued countless explorers and tourists. Today, many of these cities have become modern tourist attractions. Located on the northeast coast of the Yucatán Peninsula, Tulum is a famed town of Mayan ruins. Among the ruins is a castle-like structure that sits atop the limestone bluffs bordering the Caribbean Sea. Cancún lies a little more than 90 miles (150 km) up the coast.[8] Here, thick jungle forest reveals emerging formations of white limestone along white sand beaches. Spectacular Maya ruins rise from the beautiful surroundings. Although modern tourism has taken over much of these cities today, Maya ancestors remain throughout the Yucatán Peninsula, keeping the culture alive.

to be approximately 10,000 years old; remains from animal species now extinct; paintings and carvings depicting humans and animals; figurines and blades carved from stone; pottery; and remnants of ritualistic offerings such as snails, grain, or corn, which were often burned.

EMERGING EXPLORATION

Europeans documented cave exploration as early as the late 1300s. Baron Johann Valvasor was a famed European spelcologist who explored caves during the 1670s and 1680s. In the United States and Canada, cave study and exploration began in the 1700s and grew in the 1800s.

As cave exploration caught on, advances in techniques and equipment emerged. During early periods of caving history, candles or flaming torches provided light. Vine ladders gave way to ropes and winches. These ropes were anchored around rock formations. Rope ladders made of natural fibers and with wooden rungs were also used in early cave exploration. Helmets made of cardboard, leather, or woven bamboo were worn to protect explorers' heads from walls, ceilings, and falling rock. These rudimentary techniques and equipment remained standard in cave exploration for centuries.

SHOW CAVES

Caves used for tourism and public visitation are called show caves or commercial caves. Caves not open to the public and explored only by experienced cavers and speleologists are called wild caves. In the 1790s, a hunter stumbled upon Mammoth Cave in Kentucky, which today is recognized as the world's longest cave system at 400 miles (644 km) long. The cave's gigantic chambers led to its naming. After its discovery, African-American slave Stephen Bishop explored Mammoth Cave and acted as a tour guide for people interested in seeing it. Mammoth Cave soon became a famous show cave. The popularity of show caves rose during the Industrial Revolution and exploded in the latter part of the 1800s.

Huge numbers of caves have been found in the southeastern United States, most notably in Tennessee,

Alabama, and Georgia. These states are known collectively as TAG in the caving community. They are known to hold more than 14,000 caves, with more being discovered every year.[9]

In the southwestern United States, Carlsbad Caverns in New Mexico's Guadalupe Mountains became a famous show cave system. Carlsbad was discovered in the late 1800s, although there is debate over who was the first to explore it. Within the caves are extraordinary formations, such as the massive chamber called the Big Room. It is approximately 357,469 square feet (33,210 sq m) in area, large enough to hold more than six football fields.[10]

COMMERCIAL CAVING

Humans alter commercial caves to make them easier to enter, traverse, and examine. These alterations can include stairs, bridges, or lighting. During the 1900s, some caves were even outfitted with dining halls and dance floors. Carlsbad Caverns had a giant lunchroom installed in the 1950s. Show cave guides or organizations usually charge admission, and they present exploring the cave as a sort of tourist activity. This activity can affect cave ecosystems and scar pristine natural wonders. For this reason many in the scientific and expeditionary caving communities are dismayed by excessive cave tourism.

The Big Room in Carlsbad Caverns contains enormous features.

EARLY EXPEDITIONS

Beginning in the 1700s, depictions of caves in paintings, sketches, and engravings became popular. Photography was invented in 1839 and became the preferred medium to document scientific discoveries. However, early photographers had little success in dark caves. Filming movies in caves was also attempted beginning in the late 1800s, but lighting difficulties made many early attempts unsuccessful.

Cave archaeology began in the 1800s in Europe, with geologists and historians searching for clues about the history of the world. The popularity of exploring caves for recreation and sportsmanlike challenge rose in the late 1800s. It was influenced largely by advances in transportation technology and the expeditions of Édouard-Alfred Martel. Martel was a famed French speleologist often considered the "father of speleology."[12]

In 1902, Martel explored the Arabika Massif, a group of karst mountains found along the Black Sea in a region called Abkhazia within the Eastern European country of Georgia.

MISSION IN FOCUS
CARLSBAD CAVERNS

It is generally accepted that the official discovery of Carlsbad Caverns in New Mexico occurred in the 1800s. Throughout history, many claimed to have been the first to explore Carlsbad—none of whom were professional cavers or speleologists. One of the most famous was Jim White. White was a cowboy who became curious about a great swarming mass he witnessed coming from a hole in the ground. It was a cloud of bats, which White tracked to a cave entrance that appeared bottomless. Intrigued, he began a series of caving missions. What he experienced amazed and humbled him:

Suspended from the ceilings were mammoth chandeliers—clusters of stalactites in every size and color. . . . Floors were lost under formations of every variety and shape. . . . The beauty, the weirdness, the grandeur and the omniscience absolved my mind of all thoughts of a world above—I forgot time, place and distance. Suddenly . . . [my] flame curled up and died. It seemed as though a million tons of black wool descended upon me. The darkness was so dense it seemed smothering—choking me.[11]

White made it out of the cavern and went on to tirelessly promote its exploration. Today, Carlsbad is a national park of 118 caves, with new passages being found as recently as 2012.

The temperature on and within the massif is bone-chilling. At the time, explorers wore everyday clothing during caving exploration, layering as best they could in cold underground environments.

PROMISING DEPTHS

In 1909 and 1910, Russian scientist Alexander Kruber conducted geologic field studies in the Arabika Massif and then published his findings. The Arabika Massif lies in the Western Caucasus mountain range, which covers more than 679,540 acres (275,000 ha).[13] It is approximately eight miles (13 km) long and has elevations ranging between 5,800 and 8,000 feet (1,768 and 2,438 m).[14] Arabika is one of the largest limestone massifs within the range. Such towering heights of limestone suggest the possibility of amazingly deep caves, boring the length of the massif and into the earth below its base. Within the massif are several caves, including Krubera Cave, named after Kruber. Krubera consists of long pitches and tight meanders, and would suggest the promise of great depths to later explorers. But extensive exploration of Arabika's potentially deep caves was put on hold for approximately five decades as wars and conflicts dominated worldwide attention.

For thousands of years, caves have been used as fortresses during wars, which sometimes led to cave damage. After World War I (1914–1918), surplus cold-weather army clothing provided cavers with warmer and more durable gear for expeditions, which occurred more and more frequently in the 1920s and 1930s.

CAVING TECHNIQUES

Some basic caving techniques were established in the early 1900s, including body rappelling. This technique involves no other equipment than a doubled rope, which is weaved across a caver's body at various points: between the legs, up around the hips, across the chest, over the shoulder and then down across the back,

KRUBERA-VORONJA

Krubera is sometimes called Voronja Cave or Krubera-Voronja Cave on lists or in documents. Voronja means "crow" in Russian and is the alternative name the cave was given during 1980s explorations. The name referred to the large number of crows found nesting in the cave's entrance.

The karst landscape of the Arabika Massif provides ideal terrain for the creation of incredibly deep cave systems.

where it is gripped with his or her hand. However, it was easy for a rappeller to become separated from the rope using this technique, and cavers sought improvements.

In 1931, Austrian mountaineer Karl Prusik introduced the use of a knot that forever changed cave exploration. It was a knot sailors used at sea. The knot slid up a rope freely when unburdened with weight, but it gripped the rope tight when carrying weight. This would allow a person to inch his or her way upward by shifting weight. Prusik adapted the knot for mountaineering. Cave explorers in France often imitated mountaineers in technique and equipment at the time, and they began using Prusik knots to cave.

However, the knots were not completely successful in caving. Explorers soon discovered they would not hold tight on muddy or icy ropes. To solve this problem, small devices called mechanical ascenders were invented in 1933 to replace the knots. These devices worked similarly, sliding up when unburdened, but holding fast when weighted. Ascenders had little teeth, giving them the ability to bite down, rather than just grip, and lock securely on rope.

CAVING ADVANCES IN THE UNITED STATES

In 1941, the National Speleological Society (NSS) was established in the United States. The organization promotes the study, exploration, and conservation of caves in the United States and around the world. Today, the NSS consists of more than 250 local branches, called grottoes, and 12,000 members.[15]

In 1952, US caver Bill Cuddington created a set of techniques to ascend and descend ropes, called single rope technique (SRT). Cuddington was caving alone, which safety experts advise against. He had no problems getting down the rope using body rappelling. However, he had trouble ascending. He decided to test Prusik knots for rope ascension.

Single rope technique made it safer for cavers to get in and out of tight spaces on their own.

His trials were successful, and several techniques evolved under the SRT umbrella. These techniques are also used with ascenders. SRT caught on and continued to evolve in the 1960s.

Cavers in the United States found new areas to explore in the 1950s. They combined the latest techniques in caving and diving to explore underwater caves in Florida. Cave divers improved their equipment based on their experiences in underwater caves, and the popularity of cave exploration continued growing.

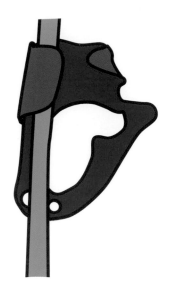

Ascender

SRT TECHNIQUES

A SRT technique often called frogging or Prusiking involves using small lengths of rope that support the feet and chest tied to the main rope with Prusik knots. One short rope attaches the caver's chest to the main rope. Two other short ropes make foot loops on the main rope. By placing feet in the foot loops, then bending and scooting the legs upward, the Prusik knot anchoring the foot loops moves up the main rope. Putting weight on the foot loops rope makes it grip the climbing rope, so the caver can extend, appearing to be in somewhat of a standing position against the length of the rope. As the caver extends his or her legs, the ascender at chest level becomes unburdened and slides easily up the main rope. Ropewalking is another SRT technique. In this method, each foot is connected separately to the main rope, one above the other, with Prusik knots. By transferring weight from one foot to the other, a caver can walk up a rope.

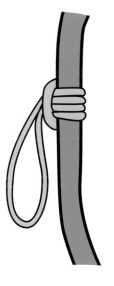

Prusik knot

USING PRUSIK KNOTS

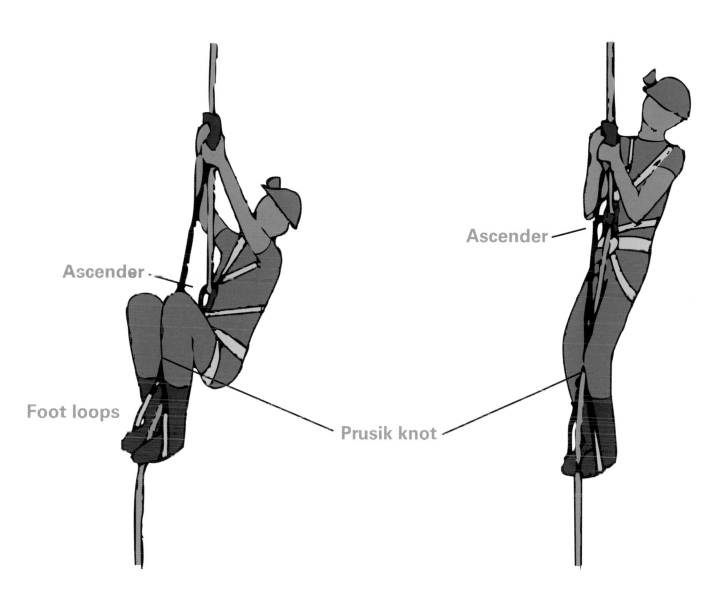

Ascender

Foot loops

Prusik knot

Ascender

Raise feet in foot loops

Stand up in foot loops and the ascender will slide up the rope

The total darkness within caves means backup flashlights are among the most critical pieces of safety equipment.

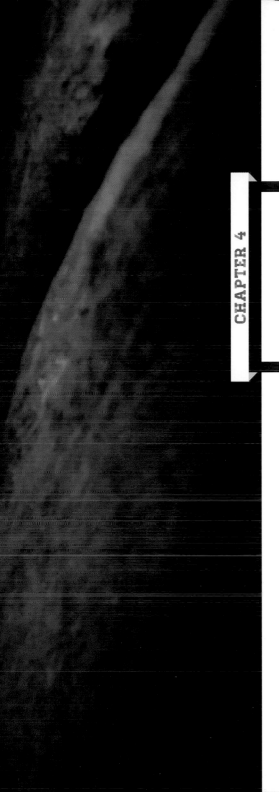

CHAPTER 4

EVOLVING EQUIPMENT AND TECHNIQUES

Caving equipment went through a period of great change and evolution throughout the 1900s. For much of the century, explorers used carbide lamps. These lamps use the chemical compound carbide to create a gas that is burned to provide an illuminating flame within a small bulb. Electric lights were also used during this time and began slowly replacing carbide lights for most cave exploration. Ladders were still used in addition to ropes in the 1960s, but

Warm clothing and high-tech helmets further enhanced caving safety and comfort.

rope ladders made of wire with aluminum rungs replaced heavy wooden versions.

The equipment used with SRT also evolved, and cavers used the techniques with more frequency. When SRT was first introduced, cavers used harnesses made for sport climbing. While sufficient, these harnesses were not ideal for cave climbing. They were uncomfortable and not perfectly suited to the environment. Specialty caving harnesses were developed. They were more comfortable during long periods of hanging in sitting positions. The new designs could also better handle abrasion and resist water, common conditions encountered in cave exploration.

In 1966, US caver John Cole created a rappel rack to make SRT descents easy to control. The device was made of bent metal and shaped to somewhat resemble an oversized paperclip, but with four to six ladderlike rungs reaching across its width. A rope is woven through the rungs

RAPPEL RACK CONFIGURATIONS

Regular Friction

Extra Friction

Locked

on the rack, providing cavers with friction and control. Different ways of threading the rope create more or less friction or set the rack in a locked position. Running the rope once through the rack creates regular friction. Running it through the rack and back again adds more friction, slowing descents. To lock it, cavers continue weaving the rope around the bars. This enables them to stop a descent. Rappel racks revolutionized caving. European cavers invented another take on an ascension device using friction for control. Known as a bobbin, the European version is a fixed pulley in which rope is woven through in an S formation. Locking mechanisms were added to bobbins in later years.

BOLTS AND BOOTS

Another major advance to equipment in the 1960s and 1970s was the development and use of rock bolts. Until this time, cavers

RIGGING A RAPPEL RACK

While rappel racks were a revolutionary cave invention, they did not guarantee safer caving. Rigging the rope through the rack in the correct way is gravely important in order to descend safely. If the rope is threaded the wrong way, the rack's bars can fly open when a caver leans back, causing him or her to fall. Cavers refer to this as "the death rig," and the subsequent fall as an "air rappel."[1] The majority of these types of falls are fatal.

used natural rock belays to anchor themselves. But the natural placement of rock belays are not always in spots that allow the safest or easiest descent. Rock bolts are small anchors permanently drilled into stone, providing solid anchors for safer long descents. Originally, explorers placed these in cave walls or ceilings using a hammer and handle, which is a pivoting steel tool used to grip and screw the bolt into the stone. Today, they are typically secured with portable hammer drills.

Caving clothing underwent changes during this era as well. Instead of everyday attire, cavers began wearing clothes used in other outdoor sports, such as woolly mountaineering undergarments, wet suits made for diving, and leather or rubber mining boots. After the 1960s, caving helmets were outfitted with special brackets designed for mining headlamps, freeing cavers' hands for rope work and exploration. The helmets were also designed to absorb shocks and became made of lightweight and durable plastic and fiberglass.

KRUBERA AND KLIMCHOUK

Throughout history, world records in size, length, and depth were the goal of many cave expeditions. Scientists showed renewed interest in the Arabika Massif in the 1960s and pushed its depths to 780 feet (238 m) in Krubera Cave. Disappointingly, Krubera narrowed to a passage too tight for human movement, and by the late 1970s explorers declared the cave did not have great depth potential. Most cavers turned elsewhere in search of record depth. However, Ukrainian caver Alexander Klimchouk remained.

Klimchouk was a caver with a scientific bent who had been interested in geology from a young age. He went on his first caving expedition in 1972 in

ALEXANDER KLIMCHOUK

Alexander Klimchouk was born in Odessa, Ukraine, in 1956. During his childhood, Klimchouk became interested in geology. He joined a group called Young Pioneers, which is similar to a mix of the Girl and Boy Scouts and the YMCA in the United States. Through the Young Pioneers, he was introduced to speleology, and his lifelong interest in caves developed. Klimchouk caved throughout college, where he earned a doctorate in hydrogeology. Sometimes called "Father Klim" by younger cavers, Klimchouk went on to establish several speleological organizations, including the Institute of Geological Sciences at the National Academy of Sciences, the Kiev Speleological Club, and the Ukrainian Speleological Association.[2]

Klimchouk embraces teammate Bernard Tourte after a successful exploration of Krubera.

what is today Uzbekistan, at the time a part of the Soviet Union. The soft-spoken Klimchouk became chairman of the Kiev Caving Commission in 1975. Four years later, in 1979, he founded the Institute of Geological Sciences at the National Academy of Sciences. By 1980, Klimchouk's passion for caving had developed in him a desire to discover the deepest cave on Earth. It was the start of a mission that would span several decades.

STONE AND SMITH

On the other side of the planet, in the United States, caver Bill Stone developed the same life mission. Stone, who had a bold personality, had also become interested in caves early in life. An avid caver throughout high school and college, Stone went on his first real expedition in 1976, to Huautla Cave in Mexico, with another US caver named Jim Smith.

The year before the 1976 Huautla expedition, Smith, an experienced caver despite being only 20 years old, had taken part in an expedition in France. There, he and the expedition team pushed the Gouffre de la Pierre Saint-Martin cave to 4,300 feet (1,310 m) deep, setting the world record for deepest cave.[3] The world record for deepest cave changed several times as cavers discovered new caves and pushed old passages to new depths. Stone and Klimchouk both longed to unearth a cave that would beat old records by a wide margin.

CRACKING SUMPS

In 1979, Stone helped lead an expedition to Huautla. The mission was to crack a sump that had stopped their search for depth on a prior expedition. Sometimes sump bottoms are closed off, and sometimes they lead to other passages. The caving term *crack a sump* describes cavers finding a way to get past a sump to continue exploring what might lie beyond it. They first attempt to pass the sump through another route, without going underwater. When that does not work, cavers use scuba diving equipment to explore and hopefully pass through the sump.

When Stone tried to crack the sump in Huautla in 1979, he had a scare in which he almost ran out of oxygen before his exploration of the sump was complete. His caving companions pulled him to safety with only a few breaths left in his air tank. This led Stone to invent his own innovative equipment in later years.

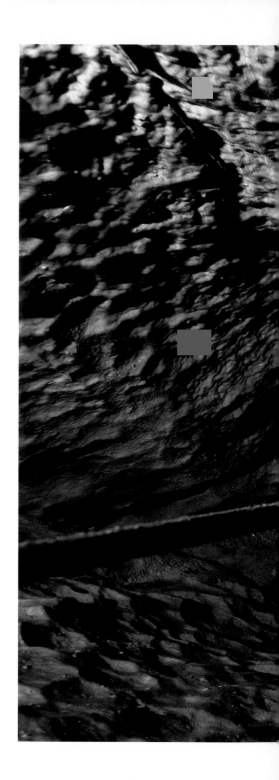

Cracking sumps is one of
the most dangerous and
rewarding parts of caving.

NO DEAD ENDS

Klimchouk continued exploring Arabika in the 1980s. Although other teams had lost faith in Arabika holding record depths, Klimchouk believed their exploration technique, not the cave itself, got in their way. He developed a methodical cave exploration style he called quicksearch. It differed from the way most cave explorers searched during expeditions. At the time, cavers and speleologists tended to look for caves and passages in obvious spots only, such as beneath great sinkholes, and not go much farther. But Klimchouk was determined to comb the entire massif inside and out carefully, using what he called a "no dead ends" approach.[4]

This was no small task. Klimchouk and his team spent three years, 1983 to 1986, clearing out a huge boulder choke in Arabika's Kujbyshevskaja Cave. The choke was filled with rocks, boulders, and freezing water, and they cleared it by hand with ropes and pulleys. It was excruciating work, but pushing though this and other chokes increased Arabika's depth to 3,500 feet (1,070 m).[5]

During expeditions in the 1980s, Klimchouk's team discovered two passage entrances that resembled windows in a wall of Krubera Cave. The team did not explore them, as they were busily pushing more obvious tunnels leading down. Instead, they decided to return and explore the windows on future trips, not knowing that it would be nearly a decade before they could do so.

ARABIKA MASSIF AND KRUBERA CAVE

Arabika Massif's highest summit reaches nearly 8,000 feet (2,438 m). The massif's landscape is spectacular and extreme, containing what one author called "emerald-green valleys and bone-white peaks and ridges, landforms so varied and chaotic they look like a storming ocean frozen in mid-tumult."[6] There are several hundred known caves in the Arabika Massif, including Krubera Cave. Krubera is thousands of feet deep and contains miles of passages. The cave passages are 90 percent vertical, and they are massive: one is 500 feet (152 m) deep.[7] The meanders connecting these pitches are often extremely tight and long, making them excruciating for some cavers. Despite having such a massive interior, Krubera's entrance is somewhat small, having been described as "about the size and shape of a big-wave surfboard."[8] Inside, the cave is extremely cold, as is the water, which is only rarely warmer than 32 degrees Fahrenheit (0°C). Airflow in the cave blows with a windchill factor below 0 degrees Fahrenheit (-18°C).[9]

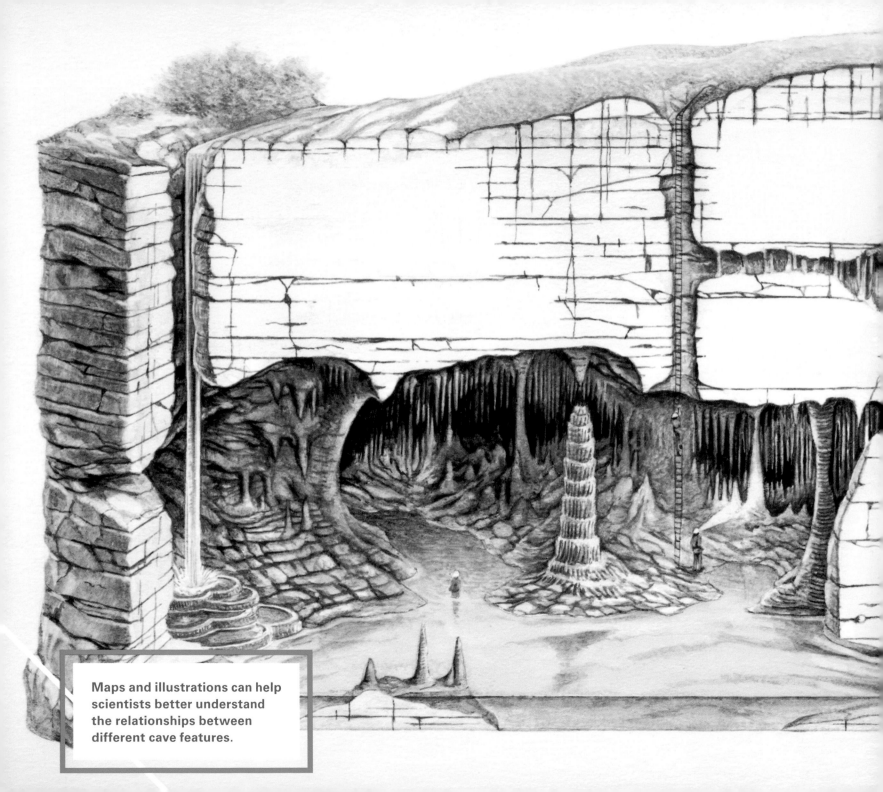

Maps and illustrations can help scientists better understand the relationships between different cave features.

CHAPTER 5

DATA, DYES, AND DISCOVERIES

Because it is impossible to see a complete cave or cave system while inside one, maps are essential for cave discovery, exploration, and study. Surveying is the gathering of information to build cave maps. Caving etiquette demands all cavers who explore virgin cave territory must also act as surveyors, carefully recording distances, elevations, passages, and terrain shapes. To do this, cavers set up several surveying stations within a cave. Then, using special instruments, they measure the new terrain. Three instruments are essential for measurement:

71

a measuring tape, a compass, and a clinometer, which measures inclination.

MAKING MAPS

A cartographer creates cave maps using computers to turn the data collected from surveying into maps detailing the cave's layout, geography, profile, and separate sections. Some cavers are also cartographers. Once cartographers make a map, they sketch in details of the cave formations and passages.

Mapmaking can take weeks, but the benefits are priceless. Sometimes a particular passage or connection will not be realized until a cave map is studied. Some cave maps are continually revised, with decades' worth of revision by several hundred different cavers.

SCOOPING BOOTY AND SURVEYING

In caving, unexplored passages are referred to as "booty."[1] *Booty* is another word for *treasure*. Exploring new territory for the first time is "scooping booty."[2] Scooping booty is considered a privilege belonging to cavers who have put the time and energy into exploring, digging, or navigating a path to the new territory. If a caver explores a new area he or she did not help discover, it is considered a great offense. Worse yet is scooping booty without going back to survey the new passages. Scooping booty is an exciting part of discovery, but cavers consider surveying most important.

The caving community often regards caving expeditions that do not lead to map additions or new maps as failures.

DYE TRACING

In 1984 and 1985, Klimchouk strengthened his conviction that Arabika held potential for great depth through dye-tracing experiments. Dye tracing is a common practice in cave exploration. One feature of surface terrain above huge cave systems is disappearing streams, which often resurface at lower elevations. Cave explorers use dyes to test what water systems connect within, above, and below caves. A dark orange

DETECTING DYE

Using dye to learn how karst waters are connected has been a practice for many years. The earliest experiments were done in Europe and North America in the early 1900s, though most experiments occurred after the 1950s. Early tests used visual traces of dye to confirm connectedness. Researchers made advances in the 1960s using carbon detectors that identify even tiny traces of the dye, as visible traces of fluorescein dye dissolve almost immediately in water.

Carbon detectors today are usually small envelopes of plastic screening that contain small amounts of activated carbon, a form of carbon packed with tiny holes. The longer the dye is exposed to the activated carbon, the greater its concentration. This allows researchers to detect small traces that cannot be seen in water by the naked eye. Balls of unbleached cotton are also sometimes used in this way.

powder called fluorescein dye is a common material used in these tests.

To test Arabika, Klimchouk poured fluorescein dye into several of the massif's cave waters, including in Krubera. He detected traces of the dye in water at lower elevations, including in springs on the shore of the Black Sea, 8,000 feet (2,440 m) lower than the caves.[3] Later, Klimchouk managed to detect traces of the dye in water that was 400 feet (122 m) below the Black Sea's surface and many miles offshore, meaning Arabika's karst-based hydrological system was the deepest known in the world.[4]

DISCOVERING CHEVE

Across the globe, caver Smith conducted a similar test in 1990 on the Sistema Cheve cave system in Mexico, which had been opened for exploration just four years earlier. In 1986, Carol Vesely and Bill Farr, a young, adventurous couple, went to the remote Mexican forest in search of a cave to explore. They stumbled upon a huge sinkhole

Teams of scientists sometimes split up to search for dye traces.

approximately one-half mile (0.8 km) long and nearly one and one-half miles (2.4 km) wide—a sign a huge cave might be near.[5] Scanning the horizon, the couple spotted a gaping rock entrance two stories high, rimmed with jutting formations—the entrance to Cheve.

Vesely and Farr explored small sections during the trip and returned for two more visits in 1987. Features they came across included a series of waterfalls, pools of "turquoise water in bronze-colored basins," and "a face of rock like burnished gold."[6] Following caving custom, the discoverers named each passage they were the first to explore. In 1988, Vesely and Farr led a group of 17 people, including Stone, to Cheve.[7]

SISTEMA CHEVE AND CHEVE CAVE

The Sistema Cheve cave system is located in the Sierra Juárez in Oaxaca, Mexico. Cheve Cave is the largest entrance to the cave system. The shaft of the enormous cave has an initial drop of approximately 3,000 feet (914 m). But the drop is not a pitch—a continuous, open drop. Many rock formations, twists, and turns are in its path. Cheve has 90 pitches long enough to require rappels.[8] The top of the cave resembles an L shape. A second foot drops off the bottom of the L approximately 2 miles (3.2 km) after the initial drop, at a slope of approximately 10 degrees.[9] Cheve Cave's climate is fairly cool and mild, with temperatures ranging in the high 40s to low 50s in degrees Fahrenheit (8–12°C). Water temperatures are approximately the same temperature as the air.[10]

LOCALS AND LAWS

In 1989, 23 cavers, including Vesely, Farr, and Stone, went on another expedition to Cheve. They ran into immediate problems with locals, who had begun to suspect the Americans traveling there so frequently were doing so to steal gold or treasure from deep within their caves.

Local governments are sometimes skeptical of foreign cave explorers or do not want them to cave and make big discoveries on their land. Some caves are on private property and require permission from the landowner for any caver, foreign or domestic, to explore. Cave landowners worry about damage to their property or land and about a caver getting hurt during exploration and suing them. To help put landowners at ease, caving lawyers developed release forms cavers sign saying the landowner is not responsible for any physical harm the caver encounters in the cave or on the owner's land. Most cavers are respectful and want the chance to explore again, so they tread carefully in privately owned caves.

To squash locals' suspicions during the Cheve expedition, Stone showed them an informational slideshow about Cheve, explaining his intent to discover the deepest cave on Earth. He convinced them it would be an honor for Cheve to win the title. Once inside the cave, the team pushed Cheve to 4,078 feet (1,243 m) deep. At the time, an Austrian cave, Lamprechtsofen, held the world-record depth at 5,354 feet (1,632 m) deep.[11] The team was not ready to give up on Cheve yet. It would be back for several expeditions in the 1990s.

Stone and Smith went on another expedition to Cheve with Vesely and Farr in 1990. During this expedition, Smith conducted dye tests to confirm Cheve had a chance at record depth. Eight days after pouring dye into Cheve's entrance, traces appeared in the Santo Domingo River, more than 8,000 feet (2,438 m) below and

NAMING CAVE PASSAGES

Cave discoverers traditionally have the privilege of naming the caves or passages they find. This is a fun part of discovery, but is also a practical way to distinguish passages during discussion and study. The NSS suggests the cave never be given a name that might reveal its location. This protects its resources from being exploited and deters inexperienced cavers from discovering it and getting hurt during exploration.

Carefully surveying caves can make it easier for future cavers to uncover new passages.

11 miles (18 km) away from Cheve's entrance.[12] Smith and Stone were thrilled. Stone prepared an expedition for the following year, which would be the beginning of a string of many years spent searching for record depth.

Technological improvements in equipment increased the extent and duration of cave diving expeditions.

CHAPTER 6

CAVE DIVING AND CAMPING

In the early 1990s, Klimchouk's exploration of Arabika came to a halt due to political reasons. In 1990, the Soviet Union broke into 15 republics, which then broke into smaller pieces again. The Republic of Georgia broke down, and in 1992, Abkhazia Province went to war with Georgia to gain its independence. Because the regions surrounding Arabika were so hostile, foreigners stayed out—including Klimchouk.

During this time, in 1990 and 1991, Stone went on expeditions to Cheve, and then on a unique training mission in Florida in 1992. Over the years, Stone became increasingly

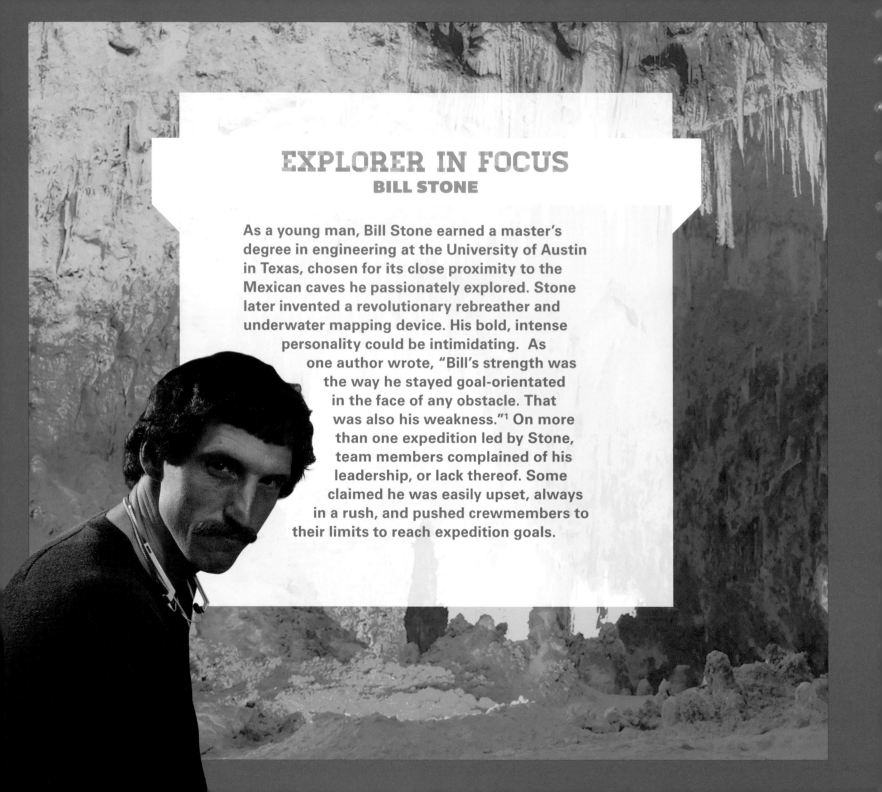

EXPLORER IN FOCUS
BILL STONE

As a young man, Bill Stone earned a master's degree in engineering at the University of Austin in Texas, chosen for its close proximity to the Mexican caves he passionately explored. Stone later invented a revolutionary rebreather and underwater mapping device. His bold, intense personality could be intimidating. As one author wrote, "Bill's strength was the way he stayed goal-orientated in the face of any obstacle. That was also his weakness."[1] On more than one expedition led by Stone, team members complained of his leadership, or lack thereof. Some claimed he was easily upset, always in a rush, and pushed crewmembers to their limits to reach expedition goals.

frustrated with air tank technology. So many times, just as cave divers would get to an unexplored portion of a sump, they would run out of air. No real headway could be made until divers could stay down longer in sumps. Stone determined to invent advanced air tanks.

He focused on special tanks called rebreathers, which US Navy divers use. Rebreathers use chemicals to scrub a diver's exhaled breath of carbon dioxide, returning it to breathable oxygen. A diver's breath can be recycled again and again for many hours, considerably longer than the approximately 20 minutes of air in a typical diving tank.[2] But navy rebreathers were not for sale for civilian use. So Stone, who holds a PhD in structural engineering, decided in 1984 to create his own. Stone refined his rebreathers

STONE'S REBREATHERS

Stone's experience in the Huautla sump in 1979 was just one of many frustrating attempts in underwater caves. When he decided to design a rebreather in 1984, he toiled in his home basement in Maryland for three years. His first version of the contraption was big and heavy. He worked on the design, miniaturized several systems, and in 1989 debuted another version. Called the MK-II, this system was 100 pounds (45 kg) lighter.[3] As he continually refined his design, Stone's rebreathers became standard in scuba and cave diving, carrying the potential to revolutionize both.

several times, and in 1992, he and a team of explorers tested an updated version for two months in Florida's underwater caves. While there, the rebreathers performed well. Stone continued to refine his rebreather, and his invention lead to a new era of cave diving exploration.

His invention a success, Stone and his team prepared to head back to Mexico and crack some sumps in 1992. However, a tragedy occurred before they left Florida. One of the training cavers lost his life underwater. The mental stresses of underwater caving caused him to panic and drown, even though he had a full air supply and functioning equipment.

CAVE DIVING DANGERS

When diving in caves, there is not always an easy escape. A cave diver may be hundreds of feet deep, with nothing overhead but a ceiling of stone. These ceilings may come crashing down suddenly. Passages may become so narrow they snag or damage equipment. Many sumps are

Awareness of surroundings is key to safety while diving in underwater caverns.

MARTINI'S LAW

Nitrogen narcosis usually occurs at depths of more than 100 feet (30 m).[5] The deeper divers go, the more likely the condition is to occur. This is because water pressure increases with depth, which also causes higher amounts of nitrogen gas, naturally found in human blood and tissues, to dissolve. This creates a feeling of dizziness or euphoria often equated to drunkenness. Martini's Law is a guideline that predicts or measures this effect. The law states that for each 50 feet (15 m) of depth, a diver will feel as they would after drinking one martini—an alcoholic drink—on an empty stomach.[6] So, 100 feet (30 m) would equate two martinis, and so on.[7]

The effects of Martini's Law can lead cave divers to act irresponsibly or strangely. There have been reports of divers trying to give their equipment to fish or just swimming away from their gear. However, cavers often recognize the signs of nitrogen narcosis before reaching this point. If a diver does notice effects, ascending usually makes the condition go away.

pitch-black. Handheld underwater lights illuminate only limited distances, making it easy to get lost or disoriented. Silt-outs, which occur when great clouds of fine silt are stirred up by cave divers' movements or contact with walls in tight squeezes, can lower visibility to a few inches, which can be disorienting.

Perhaps the most treacherous element of cave diving is the mental issues it can cause. One example is nitrogen narcosis, which is also known as "the rapture of the deep."[4] Divers experience this due to too much nitrogen in their systems, making them dizzy, disoriented, and confused. High-pressure nervous syndrome (HPNS) is another danger. HPNS is a neurological reaction to extremely high pressure that causes physical affects such as body convulsions and hallucinations.

CAVE DIVING TRAINING AND SAFETY

Cave divers prepare through classes, certification, and safety checks. Two levels of cave-diving certification exist. In the first, the caver is not allowed to dive below certain depths and distances, keeping the sump entrance in sight at all times. At this level, cavers must pass a series of safety drills to move to the next level. These tests include laying out a guideline and exiting a cave by touch only, without any light. Only a small percentage of cave divers pass to the second level.

A guideline, usually made of nylon twine, is a cave diver's lifeline. Kept in hand on a spooled reel during the dive, cave divers secure the guideline frequently at points along the center of a passage so they can follow it back. This also provides a way of measuring an underwater cave. Divers record each spot where the line is tied off using a waterproof slate and then calculate totals after surfacing.

In addition to goggles, helmets, lights, and fins, divers also use buoyancy compensators, which help them float on the surface with all their heavy gear or keep them neutrally buoyant at great depths, where pressure can alter buoyancy. Other cave diving equipment includes air tanks or rebreathers, which are usually strapped to cave divers' sides in harnesses to allow passage through tight underwater squeezes. A spare air supply and regulator are also standard in cave dives. A "rule of thirds" calls for cave divers to stop exploring when they have used one-third of their air supply. They save the other two-thirds to ensure they can make the trip back out of the sump.[8]

Assembling and checking all of this equipment before a caver dives can be quite a task. Ian Rolland and Kenny Broad, cave divers on

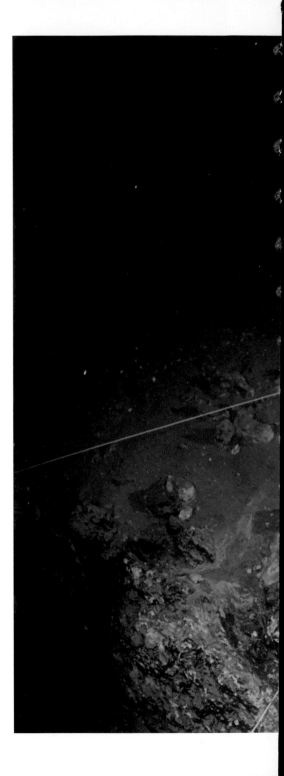

Some cave divers use
specialized mapping
equipment to chart
the underwater caves
they explore.

Stone's 1994 Huautla expedition, went through three pages of checklists before diving a sump. The expedition that year had its share of challenges outside the water as well.

Stone's goal for the 1994 Huautla expedition was to break through a difficult sump that had blocked them from a passage since 1979. For two weeks, the team worked its way deeper into the cave, hauling down supplies. Staying below ground for two weeks is not uncommon during a caving expedition—but it is not always easy or pleasant.

CAVE CAMPING

When camping in a cave, it is always absolutely dark. Eating, sleeping, cooking, going to the bathroom, and waking up are often done in complete darkness.

UNDERWATER CAVE MAPPING

In 1998, Stone worked on a project to map the Wakulla Springs underwater cave system in Florida. This gave him the chance to refine his rebreathers yet again and to test out another invention he had created: a system using computers and sonar to create three-dimensional underwater maps in color. After three months, the project, called the Wakulla Springs Mapping Project, produced the first fully three-dimensional cave map. Thirty-two sonar transducers had collected millions of data points, accurately scanning and measuring every inch of the underwater caves. It was an incredible feat in the world of mapping natural structures.

Cavers do have lights, but they try to save their batteries or carbide for exploration.

Because everything used must be hauled down on ropes or cavers' backs, the weight of supplies is always important to cavers, who have turned cutting weight and paring down supplies into a science. Whole expedition teams will often use one pot, one bowl, and one utensil—shared by everyone—to cook and eat with during an expedition. One caver will eat from the bowl and pass it to the next, who will use the same spoon or fork, and so on.

Finding a comfortable, safe place to sleep in a cave can be a challenge. Often the only place to spread out is among boulders, using wet suits as padding for beds. Sometimes only vertical walls are available, so cavers drill hammocks into the walls. Sleeping does not always come easy. Caves are often quite noisy, with rushing waterfalls or rivers nearby that never let up.

The cavers camping in Huautla in 1994 endured many of these challenges and then some. Tragedy hit when Rolland died while diving a sump. Many members quit,

Camping in ice caves carries its own challenges, such as keeping warm while sleeping.

overwhelmed by grief and exhaustion. Just two cavers stayed on with Stone. The expedition led to the discovery of seven new sumps and a lot of new territory, pushing Huautla to 4,839 feet (1,475 m) deep and reestablishing it as the deepest cave in North America.[9] But it was still not the deepest in the world.

Stone continued refining his rebreather in the 1990s. Other technology had advanced as well, and a group of filmmakers was preparing expeditions that would give people a spectacular look at the world underground.

Glacier caves are sometimes brighter than stone caves, but they carry their own special dangers.

CHAPTER 7

EXTREME ENVIRONMENTS

wo women stood atop a slippery ledge on a mountain of ice as tall as a skyscraper. Plunging below them, a frigid river sloshed, surrounded by jutting glacial formations. The cavers, Hazel Barton and Nancy Holler Aulenbach, gazed to the spot where the icy river disappeared into a frozen cave 700 feet (213 m) deep. They prepared to traverse the icy landscape to enter the cave by dangling from a nylon rope. If a spray of water hit them, they could die in minutes—the water was so cold it could quickly cause hypothermia. The spray of the frigid water also released tiny ice crystals into the air which could damage their lungs and cause suffocation.

Unlike stone caves, some glacier caves have the advantage of light, provided by the bright blue of the icy walls lit from the outside by the sun. But Barton and Aulenbach were used to dropping into pits shrouded in complete darkness, and the light was not reassuring. The massive depth—and the possibility of falling into it—remained visually apparent.

FILMED EXPEDITIONS

In the late 1990s and early 2000s, a group of cavers went on expeditions in three very different cave environments. Exploration locales included frigid glacier caves in Greenland in 1998, deep underwater caves in Mexico's

GLACIER CAVES VERSUS ICE CAVES

Glacier caves and ice caves are not the same. Glacier caves are the hollow caverns and passages formed within glaciers or between glaciers and their base contact with rock below. Ice caves are caves that have formations of ice within their walls year-round. These formations can begin as sheets of ice, and ice stalactites and stalagmites, which usually melt in warmer seasons. If temperatures do not increase, these ice formations become permanent and take the form of ice blocks. The world's largest ice cave is Austria's Eisriesenwelt, or "World of the Ice Giants."[1]

Huge caves are located at the bottom of the Grand Canyon in Arizona.

Yucatán Peninsula in 1999, and caves in the sheer cliff walls
of Arizona's massive canyons in 2000.

These expeditions were filmed and the footage
turned into the film *Journey into Amazing Caves*. The film
was presented in the colossal widescreen IMAX format,
providing theater viewers with an unprecedented look at the
unique worlds thriving beneath them.

GLACIER CAVING

Glacier caves are constantly changing due to sun and pressure. Sun can melt the surface of the glacier, creating new torrents of meltwater that freeze and change passages' shape overnight. Freezing sprays of water within the caves can also change passage shapes. Cavers may anchor ropes only to find them frozen over the next day. Setting anchors is a dangerous feat in a glacier cave. Each crack of a hammer or hatchet could cause chunks of the ice wall to break off and fall. However, the ice may also crack and break off without cavers' interference, as the cave walls naturally shift under the great pressure and weight of the glacier, sending massive hunks of jagged ice flying with a loud crack.

Capturing the beauty and danger of this extreme cave environment was an overarching goal of the filmed expeditions, but the expeditionary teams had scientific and exploratory goals

GREENLAND'S ICE CAP

The majority of Greenland lies in the Arctic Circle and is covered with a massively thick sheet of ice called a continental glacier. The ice is very thick, measuring more than 10,000 feet (3,000 m) in some places. Glacier caves are located within this thick ice sheet.

EXPLORER IN FOCUS
HAZEL BARTON

Hazel Barton is a woman of many scientific, adventurous pursuits. Born in Bristol, England, in 1971, Barton began caving when she was 16. She has chaired the Colorado Grotto and the Rocky Mountain region cave survey and was elected to the NSS Board of Governors in May 2000. Barton has a PhD in microbiology, which she applied to the study of cave microbes. She is also a talented cave cartographer, and her maps have won many awards.

for each mission as well. Barton and Aulenbach were both 27 years old during the Greenland expedition in September 1998, and both were experienced cavers. Barton is also a microbiologist. Her goal for the three expeditions was to capture and study cave microbes, which are microscopic organisms. Some cave microbes play a role in forming caves and speleothems by depositing minerals or dissolving rock. Most microbes' function in caves is to cycle nutrients to organisms higher on the food chain. Certain microbes may also produce vitamins for these organisms.

TROGLOBITES AND EXTREMOPHILES

Troglobites are organisms adapted to living underground for their entire lives—they cannot survive outside their cave environments and have never seen sunlight. Troglobites include types of crustaceans, fish, insects, salamanders, snails, and worms. Cave microbes can also be considered troglobites, but they fall into another category as well: extremophiles.

The blind grotto salamander lives in many US caves.

Extremophiles are organisms that survive in extreme environments, such as complete darkness, high pressure, and frigid temperatures. Extremophile cave microbes depend on the chemical conversion of minerals to survive, rather than sunlight and more conventional foods. Areas where two types of chemistry meet are where the richest concentrations of microbes are found. These areas include layers of two types of rock, ice, or water.

Scientists such as Barton hope studying unknown cave microbes will lead to great discoveries valuable to human life. The chemical reactions associated with the world's microbes are useful to humans in medicine. Penicillin is one example. It is created by a natural defense in a cheese mold and can be employed to kill diseases and infections. Scientists believe unique extremophile microbes might also provide new drugs or insights in medical research and treatments. The possibilities are endless, as cave microbes are extremely varied around the world, even within particular caves.

Many cave microbes are one-celled organisms. Within the Greenland glacier cave, however, Barton also studied tardigrades. These organisms can be seen only under a microscope and have blood, brains, and an immune system. Tardigrades' unique blood allows them to endure extreme

TARDIGRADE BLOOD

Tardigrades' blood allows them to survive continual freezing and thawing. Researchers have determined how. In all living organisms, there is water in and around cells. If the organism gets too cold, the water around these cells freezes and forms into large ice crystals. These large crystals rupture the membranes of the cells, causing them to die.

Tardigrades' blood has special molecules that encourage small ice-crystal growth. These crystals are not large enough to damage cells. When temperatures get cold, most of the water in tardigrades' cells has already formed into small ice crystals, so there is not enough water to form large ice crystals, meaning their cells remain unharmed. Tardigrades also have the ability to produce a type of personal antifreeze that slows the freezing process and stabilizes cell membranes as they freeze, preventing damage.

cold. A tardigrade can freeze solid with no metabolic activity—a state called cryptobiosis—and come back to life once it thaws. Studying the way tardigrades do this could be beneficial to human medical research. The next filmed expedition, set for the fall of 1999, was slated to allow Barton to study microbes in a much warmer environment.

KASJAN AND KRUBERA

In August 1999, Ukrainian cavers returned to Arabika. Klimchouk's organization, the Ukrainian Speleological Association, planned the expedition, but Klimchouk did not attend. He did not always lead or even go on the caving expeditions he planned, instead acting as organizer from afar so the next generation of cavers and speleologists could inherit established exploring techniques, improve on them, and pass them on. A 38-year-old Ukrainian caver named Yury Kasjan led the expedition that year as well as several that followed. Kasjan has a degree in geology and dreamed of adventure while growing up, which he fulfilled through caving.

Expeditions to Krubera usually establish a base camp near the cave entrance.

The goal of the 1999 Arabika expedition was to explore the two window-like passages that had been found but not pushed in the 1980s. The first ended in a closed chamber that did not extend Krubera's depth. The other extended into a tunnel and pit that led to the remainder of Krubera's passages. It was a major turning point and pushed the cave to nearly 2,500 feet (762 m). The team stopped there only because it ran out of supplies and rope. It would have to plan another expedition to continue the push.

YUCATÁN CENOTES

In the fall of 1999, the second IMAX film expedition was underway in the cenotes of the Yucatán Peninsula. Cenotes are vertical, caved-in limestone sinkholes filled with water. Eons ago, the cenotes in the Yucatán were dry caves where breathtaking calcite stalactites and stalagmites, draperies, and columns formed. Approximately 10,000 years ago, the sea level rose and water filled the caves. The calcite formations remained, creating a beautiful underwater labyrinth of stone. In an aerial view of the surface, cenotes resemble giant potholes filled with bright blue water among thick jungle.

The Yucatán cenotes are mostly freshwater. However, salt water seeps in from the nearby Caribbean coast as well, creating a mixing zone called a halocline. The melding of freshwater and saltwater chemistries creates a shimmering, floating layer that produces the illusion of air and water, or water and oil, meeting.

The halocline was where Barton hoped to collect microbe samples during the 1999 expedition. Because microbes feed off of chemical reactions, the meeting of the two water chemistries is a potential hot zone for microbe activity. Barton's research was the first time a trained microbiologist would study a halocline and its possible microbe life. It was also the first time the halocline had ever been successfully captured on film. The hazy halocline and sparkling underwater speleothems of the cenotes were soon replaced by dizzying height and dusty red rock cliffs for the last leg of the documented expeditions.

Some cenotes have become popular tourist sites.

The caves in the limestone cliffs of Arizona are notoriously difficult to access.

CHAPTER 8

SCALING HEIGHTS, DIGGING DEEPER

It was May 2000. The temperature stood at a scorching 112 degrees Fahrenheit (44°C). Cavers balanced on a cliff ledge of crumbling rock 2,000 feet (610 m) high, overlooking the Little Colorado River. The group was just upstream from where the Marble Canyon ends and the Grand Canyon begins in Arizona. Along the sheer cliff of Redwall limestone was the entrance to a cave that had never been explored because its towering elevation made it so difficult to reach. Aulenbach rappelled 300 feet (91 m) down the vertical rock face. Once she arrived at the entrance, she swung inside.

Before filming this expedition, some of the IMAX film crew had determined Greenland's glacier cave had presented the most treacherous conditions they had ever encountered. But after filming on the plummeting, exposed cliff ledges in Arizona, they changed their minds.

SOUTHWESTERN MARVELS

In the late 1860s and early 1870s, John Wesley Powell surveyed unexplored land in the Grand Canyon and published a book detailing his expeditions. Powell's descriptions of the canyon and of the magnificent caves within it were poetic and often accurate, but he moved dates and locations and altered events for the sake of telling a good story. This caused much controversy in the field, but it piqued the public's interest and lent the area's caves an air of mystery from then on. The caves are still often treated somewhat

GRAND CANYON, MARBLE CANYON

The Grand Canyon is located in northern Arizona. At its lowest point, the canyon is approximately 6,000 feet (1,800 m) deep. It is approximately 277 miles (446 km) long, and it ranges from 175 yards (160 m) to 18 miles (29 km) wide.[1] Marble Canyon begins at the northeastern end of the Grand Canyon's path within Grand Canyon National Park. The Colorado River carved both canyons.

Carlsbad Caverns is equipped to accommodate tourists. It even features an underground souvenir shop.

like secrets that are to be shared only between local cavers. Getting permission to explore these mysterious locales for the film was thrilling to the expedition's nonlocal cavers, such as Aulenbach, who was a native TAG caver.

The southwestern United States is home to many other unique caves, such as Lechuguilla Cave within Carlsbad Caverns National Park in New Mexico. The caves of Carlsbad were carved from the bottom up by sulfuric acid. Lechuguilla has especially high concentrations of sulfur deposits and the mineral gypsum, which create rare speleothems. Formations within Lechuguilla include long, delicate branches of crystals reaching 20 feet (6 m) long, small spheres of calcite called cave pearls, and more.[2]

TROGLOPHILES AND TROGLOXENES

Although home to a host of rare formations, Lechuguilla does not have much life besides cave microbes. Cave crickets and spiders have been found near the cave's entrance, but not much else.

There are 118 caves total that make up Carlsbad Caverns, and within many are bustling habitats.[3] The caves have several species of troglophiles, organisms that can live either full-time in or outside a cave. Cave troglophiles include beetles, earthworms, salamanders, and spiders. Animals that cannot survive full-time in caves but

FRAGILE FORMATIONS

The formations of Lechuguilla are so fragile the cave is the most restricted cave on Earth. Only those with serious scientific research or mapping work are allowed inside. One geologist predicted if Lechuguilla was opened to the public, the moisture and shifts in air patterns might be enough to cause delicate formations to crash from the walls and ceilings.

live in them part-time or visit them are called trogloxenes. These animals include bats, bears, rodents, snakes, and many types of birds. Some trogloxenes leave caves only to feed, such as bats. Others enter the cave only to nest or hibernate in places where winters are cold.

FIRST LOOK

Rappelling in the burning canyon heat, Barton met Aulenbach in the entrance chamber of the canyon cave, later named IMAX Cave. Barton did something many cavers do when entering a new passage: she raised her hand in the air. The presence of a breeze will tell the caver if a passage continues, and the strength of the wind can help them estimate the size of possible caves or passages beyond. Barton felt a strong breeze in the canyon cave, which picked up as she moved further in the passage. But before they could explore further, the film crew called them back to the cave entrance to do some shots for the film.

During the expedition, Barton was able to gather samples of microbes for future study. The team caught their first looks at the towering, mysterious caves of the dusty desert canyons on film. Meanwhile, the search for the deepest cave on Earth was heating up.

RACE TO THE CENTER OF THE EARTH

In August 2000, Klimchouk sent another Kasjan-led expedition to Arabika. The team pushed the cave to 3,888 feet (1,185 m). The cavers left their rope systems in place, and at the end of the month, another team arrived in a back-to-back expedition that would push Krubera to 4,600 feet (1,402 m).[4] A tight passage stopped them from going further. But they also discovered another window in the cave wall at these new depths, and the air coming from behind it was promising. The team was excited, but it was also out of supplies. Rather than wait until the following summer for warmer conditions, another expedition for the upcoming winter was quickly planned.

In the winter of 2000–2001, Klimchouk again organized a Kasjan-led expedition to Arabika. The team set off

Some of Krubera's passages had to be cleared of rocks before the explorers could pass.

on Christmas Day 2000. They penetrated the window discovered over the summer and pushed the cave an additional 156 feet (48 m), making it to 4,756 feet (1,450 m). At the time, the deepest cave in the world was still Lamprechtsofen at 5,354 feet (1,327 m). The team pushed on, and on January 4, 2001, they explored Krubera Cave to 5,510 feet (1,679 m), making it the deepest-known cave on Earth. Klimchouk and the team were thrilled, but they had actually expected the cave would have gone much deeper, by perhaps 1,000 feet (305 m) or so.[5]

Although Klimchouk and Kasjan felt Krubera had deeper potential, pushing the cave so deep in such a short time was monumental in the caving world. The Krubera team beat the world record by 250 feet (76 m) in one expedition, which was nearly unheard of. For the past 30 years,

THE DEEPEST-KNOWN SPOT ON EARTH

The spot reached in Krubera in 2001 was discovered in a triangular-shaped chamber found at the bottom of several vertical pitches. In the floor of this chamber was a small, shallow crater approximately three feet (1 m) wide and two feet (0.6 m) deep. The base of this crater came to a point where a small white rock sat. The depth was measured all the way to the bottom of that rock.

depth advances pushed an average of less than 50 feet (15 m) per year. Additionally, Krubera's recognition as the world's deepest cave represented the first time in history a cave outside Western Europe earned the title. Science and caving societies worldwide gave the team great praise for all of these accomplishments.

The Krubera record did not mean the competition, which *National Geographic* called "racing to the center of the earth" in later years, was over.[6] Stone continued pushing Mexican caves to beat the record, shifting his focus from Huautla back to Cheve. Like the rest of the worldwide caving community, he had heard of the Krubera feat. But Stone had also heard the team had plans to continue pushing the cave, hoping for even greater depth. Stone would do the same in Mexico, feeling even more pressure to take the lead.

Klimchouk and his teams continued to push Krubera deeper and deeper.

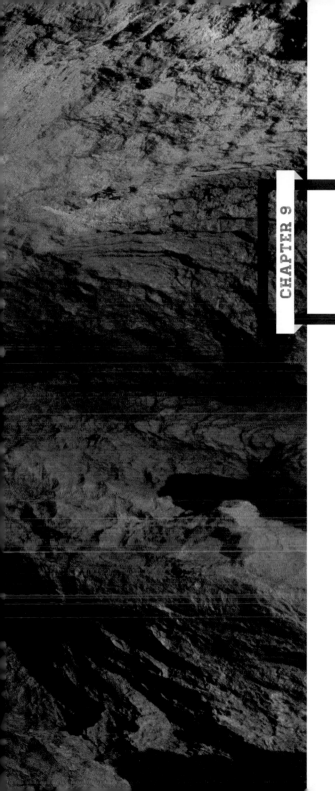

CHAPTER 9

UNDERGROUND ADVENTURES TODAY

In February 2001, Klimchouk formed a new goal: discovering the first cave 6,562 feet (2,000 m) deep. This would be 1,000 feet (305 m) deeper than the record depth his expedition had just established in Krubera. Before the most recent Krubera expedition, caving explorers around the world had collectively taken 25 years to extend the world record by 1,000 feet (305 m). Klimchouk would try to do it again in just a few years, drawing criticism from some of his contemporaries. He called his new venture the Call of the Abyss Project.

GAME OVER

As Klimchouk focused on his new goal, Stone went on expeditions to Cheve in 2003 and 2004. Although they pushed the cave a bit deeper, his teams did not hit record-breaking depths. Klimchouk's team reinforced Krubera's title as the world's deepest cave in August 2004, pushing it to 6,037 feet (1,840 m) deep. However, this was still short of his goal. The following October, Klimchouk organized an expedition led by Kasjan. After days of exploration, the team pushed the cave deeper, but did not reach the depths sought by Klimchouk. The team took a day to rest. And then, extreme depth was achieved.

"Two thousand and eighty meters [6,825 feet]," Kasjan announced upon measuring the deepest-known cave on Earth.[1] The expedition team burst into cheers. It had possibly just witnessed the last great terrestrial discovery. It was the first time in history a cave of more than 6,562 feet (2,000 meters) had been discovered and explored.[2] The team named the location Game Over.

CONTINUED EXPLORATION

The Call of the Abyss Project continued, and teams pushed Krubera's depth bit by bit between 2004 and 2006, ending at 7,188 feet (2,191 m) deep.[3] Others made caving records and discoveries in the early 2000s as well. A 2009–2010 expedition in Vietnam established Han Son Doong as the world's largest cave passage. The massive, continuous passage is approximately 300 feet (91 m) wide and more than 600 feet (183 m) high.[4]

In May 2012, an expedition in Lechuguilla unlocked a new section of passages, chambers, and pits the team named Oz. That August, Krubera made news yet again when its depths were pushed to 7,208 feet (2,197 m) deep.[5] That same month, another expedition pushed Sarma Cave, also in the Arabika Massif, to 6,004 feet (1,830 m), making it the

SECRET CAVES

Arizona cavers are especially secretive with their caves. The state's cavers have a motto: "Arizona has no caves to speak of."[6] When it comes to publishing photographs or articles featuring Arizona caves, natives usually do so only if obtaining government protection is involved or to reveal a scientific discovery to the world. But even in published accounts, Arizona cavers will often use vague descriptions to somewhat veil the cave's location.

Cavers are still making incredible discoveries and charting new caverns across the world.

world's second-deepest cave. Many expect it will not be the last cave record set in the region.

SECRETS AND SPELUNKERS

Great discoveries and visually stunning films and photos have incited awe and increased awareness of Earth's last great frontier. But while some cavers believe the attention is needed to boost conservation efforts, others feel increased interest equals potential damage to caves and cave organizations. Noncavers who seek unsupervised trips into caves are met with distrust and dismay by most cavers. In fact, it is a caving community custom to keep noncavers in the dark regarding cave locations. This includes the general public and spelunkers.

Many people use the term *spelunker* to describe cave explorers, but this is incorrect and somewhat offensive to many of today's cavers. Cave explorers have not referred to themselves as spelunkers for approximately 50 years. Today, they prefer the term *caver.* To cavers, a spelunker is considered someone who caves recreationally, with little to no experience, and without serious scientific or exploratory goals.

Cavers protect caves from casual visitors for several reasons. Many caves are located on private property. The caving community has worked hard to establish good relationships with private owners, and both they and the owners generally do not want irresponsible, disrespectful noncavers exploring on their property. Inexperienced or recreational explorers are more likely to get lost, hurt, or even killed in wild caves. And those who are uneducated or do not care about the cave might also damage delicate formations or ecosystems, either on accident or on purpose. Some caves have been vandalized with litter, spray paint, and carvings.

The camaraderie between cave explorers binds them together through fierce competition and dark, dangerous spaces.

MISSION IN FOCUS
CAVE OF CRYSTALS

While scouring the Naica mine in northern Mexico for lead in 2000, two brothers stumbled upon something much greater. At approximately 1,000 feet (300 m) below the surface, the brothers accidentally broke through the mine wall they were drilling.[7] On the other side, they discovered a labyrinth of colossal crystals—some more than 30 feet (9 m) long—stacked in what became known as Cueva de los Cristales, or Cave of Crystals.[8] When scientists explored the cave, they were amazed—and nearly killed by the extreme environment. The cave's temperature hovers around 120 degrees Fahrenheit (50°C) and has a near 100-percent humidity level. Breathing in the air causes fluid to condense in the lungs, and the temperature can cause heatstroke. The first cavers to explore the cave escaped on the verge of unconsciousness. Subsequent explorers wore cooling suits and breathing masks.

Still, exploration usually averaged no more than 20 minutes even in such protective gear.[9] The extreme climate of the cave caused the minerals in the water to evaporate and form into crystals, which grew to massive size. When miners nearby drained the water, the huge crystals were exposed.

CAVE RESTORATION AND CAVER CAMARADERIE

Damage from recreational or inexperienced cavers, tourists, or vandals is cleaned up through the efforts of cave restoration projects. Before restoration begins, conservationists evaluate the entire cave environment and carefully develop a restoration plan. The main goal is to not cause the cave any additional harm. Caving groups donate much time, energy, and money to cleaning up and restoring caves and karst landscapes. Restoration can include cleaning up debris, spray paint, and garbage, and repairing damaged speleothems or working to restore damaged habitats. Sometimes restoration includes returning a former show cave to its wild, pristine state.

HOW TO PROPERLY INQUIRE ABOUT CAVING

Cavers are trained to be protective of cave locales, even if it means being downright rude to those inquiring. To people who are seriously interested in becoming a caver, contacting an organization such as the National Speleological Society (NSS) is most helpful. Although the NSS will not point newcomers in the direction of a wild cave, the organization is a good place to gain experience and knowledge. If the transition to serious, experienced caver is completed, caving culture expects the caver to follow its rules. As one caver put it, "You're a caver now, and you have your rude responsibilities."[10]

In addition to a collective concern for the well-being of caves, cavers share a camaraderie that forms through a collective passion for spending weeks on end hanging on ropes and navigating mud, water, slime, and rock in the pitch-black darkness in the name of discovery. Many serious cavers move to live in cave-rich areas, such as TAG. Cave exploration takes a strong will, brave attitude, and powerful perseverance. As Stone explains it:

> You might as well go home if you aren't prepared to stick it out under the worst imaginable conditions for far longer than it was initially interesting or comfortable. Only then do you cross the threshold into being a real explorer with the determination to see something epic happen.[11]

TIMELINE

35,000 BCE Ancient humans use caves as dwellings, leaving behind artifacts and primitive yet revealing cave artwork.

1500 BCE The Maya people, whose culture centered on caves, emerge in the Yucatán Peninsula in Mexico.

1300s CE Early caving explorations are documented in Europe.

1700–1800s Cave exploration develops and rises in popularity in parts of North America. Many caves are turned into show caves.

1800s–1900s Exploring caves for recreation and challenge grows, influenced by French speleologist Édouard-Alfred Martel.

EARLY 1900s Caving equipment and techniques evolve, including body rappelling, Prusik knots, and ascenders.

MIDDLE 1900s Single rope technique and cave diving are established; caving gear continues to become specialized, including harnesses, helmets, rock bolts, and rappel racks.

1980s Klimchouk develops his "no dead ends" approach and pushes Arabika's Kujbyshevskaja Cave to 3,500 feet (1,070 m) deep.

1984–1985 Klimchouk conducts dye-tracing experiments, proving Arabika's potential for great depth.

1990 Bill Stone, Jim Smith, and other expedition members confirm through a dye-tracing experiment that Cheve cave holds potential for world-record depth.

1994 Stone pushes Huautla cave in Mexico to 4,839 feet (1,475 m), making it North America's deepest cave.

1998 The IMAX film and caving crew for *Journey into Amazing Caves* explores Greenland's glacier caves and their unique microbes in September.

2001 In January, Kasjan and Klimchouk's team pushes Krubera to 5,510 feet (1,679 m), making it the world's deepest-known cave.

2003–2004 Stone goes on expeditions to Cheve, and pushes its depth, but not enough to take the world record.

2004 Krubera becomes the first-known cave deeper than 6,562 feet (2,000 m)—reaching 6,825 feet (2,080 m)—in October.

2009–2010 An expedition in Vietnam establishes Han Son Doong as the world's largest cave chamber.

2012 In August, cavers push Krubera to a new depth of 7,208 feet (2,197 m).

ESSENTIAL FACTS ABOUT CAVE EXPLORATION

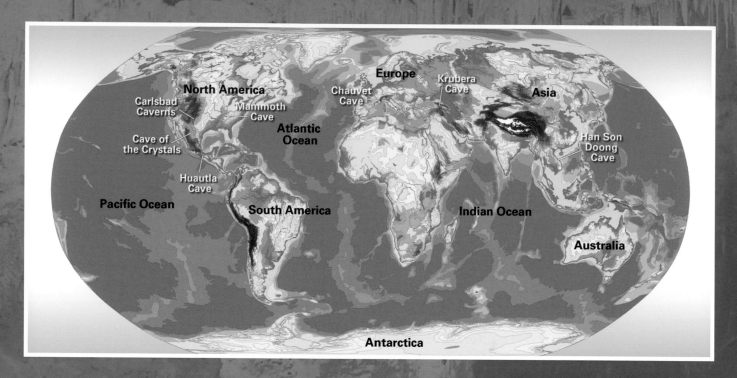

KEY DISCOVERIES AND THEIR IMPACT

Cave exploration rose in popularity in the 1700s and 1800s as desire and means of travel grew. The development of specific techniques and specialized caving equipment in the 1900s revolutionized caving, and the field carved its own niche in the realm of exploration.

In 2001, a team led by Ukrainian caver Yury Kasjan and organized by Klimchouk pushes Krubera Cave in the Arabika Massif to 5,510 feet (1,679 m). The achievement cements Krubera's title as the world's deepest-known cave.

KEY PLAYERS

Édouard-Alfred Martel is known as the "father of speleology."

Alexander Klimchouk is the caver and speleologist behind the discovery of the world's first-known cave 6,562 feet (2,000 m) deep.

Bill Stone is a persevering cave expedition leader who revolutionized cave diving with his invention of a refined rebreather and underwater three-dimensional cave mapping device.

Hazel Barton is a caver and microbiologist who studies cave microbes in the hope of making valuable medical research discoveries.

KEY TECHNOLOGY

Ascenders, rappel racks, and rock bolts made it easier and safer for cavers to lower themselves into vertical cave passages and climb back up.

Lighted helmets and flashlights gave cavers clearer views of caves. Backup light sources added an extra layer of safety in totally dark underground caverns.

Rebreathers made it possible to explore and pass through flooded passages.

QUOTE

"You might as well go home if you aren't prepared to stick it out under the worst imaginable conditions for far longer than it was initially interesting or comfortable. Only then do you cross the threshold into being a real explorer with the determination to see something epic happen."

—Bill Stone

GLOSSARY

aquifer
A geologic formation that holds water.

artifact
Something created by humans, especially a tool or weapon.

ascending
Rising or climbing.

belay
The activity of anchoring a rope on a rock or bolt, or the place where a belaying climber is anchored.

camaraderie
Trust, friendliness, and good relations with another person or group of people.

caving
The activity of exploring a cave.

hypothermia
Dangerously low body temperature.

ice cap
A thick sheet of ice covering a large area of land.

massif
A tight mass of mountains.

rappelling
Wrapping a rope around the body to slow a descent from a cliff face or into a cave to a safe speed.

rudimentary
Limited or basic.

ruins
The remains of something destroyed.

speleology
The science of studying caves.

spring
Water that wells up from the ground.

topography
The surface features of a place or region.

virgin territory
A cave passage that, to cavers' knowledge, no one has ever set foot in.

winch
A device that cranks rope or chain around a drum to hoist or lower heavy objects.

ADDITIONAL RESOURCES

SELECTED BIBLIOGRAPHY

"Field Dispatch: The Race to the Center of the Earth." *National Geographic.com*. National Geographic Society, 2004. Web.

Tabor, James M. *Blind Descent: The Quest to Discover the Deepest Place on Earth*. New York: Random, 2010. Print.

Taylor, Michael Ray. *Caves: Exploring Hidden Realms*. Washington, DC: National Geographic, 2000. Print.

FURTHER READINGS

Green, Dan. *Scholastic Discover More: Rocks and Minerals*. New York: Scholastic, 2013. Print.

Luhr, James F., ed. *Earth*. New York: DK, 2007. Print.

WEB SITES

To learn more about exploring caves, visit ABDO Publishing Company online at **www.abdopublishing.com**. Web sites about exploring caves are featured on our Book Links page. These links are routinely monitored and updated to provide the most current information available.

FOR MORE INFORMATION

For more information on this subject, contact or visit the following organizations:

National Park Services Cave & Karst Resources

National Park Service
1849 C Street NW
Washington, DC 20240
202-208-3818
http://www.nature.nps.gov/geology/caves
The National Park Service manages more than 4,900 caves within US national parks and offers educational materials and a hands-on program focusing on the study, conservation, and protection of caves and karst.

The National Speleological Society

2813 Cave Avenue
Huntsville, AL 35810-4431
256-852-1300
http://www.caves.org
The National Speleological Society promotes and supports the study of caves and karst, providing resources on training, education, exploration, and conservation of US caves.

SOURCE NOTES

CHAPTER 1. THE EIGHTH CONTINENT

1. James M. Tabor. *Blind Descent: The Quest to Discover the Deepest Place on Earth*. New York: Random, 2010. Print. xiv.

2. Ibid. 123.

CHAPTER 2. CAVE FORMATION AND FEATURES

1. "Geographic Distribution of Karst Terrain." *Encyclopaedia Britannica*. Encyclopaedia Britannica, 2013. Web. 5 June 2013.

2. Ibid.

3. "Cave." *Encyclopaedia Britannica*. Encyclopaedia Britannica, 2013. Web. 5 June 2013.

CHAPTER 3. CAVING HISTORY

1. "Archaeologists Find 1.4-Million-Year-Old Flint in Spain." *New Straits Times*. New Straits Times, 25 July 2013. Web. 9 Sept. 2013.

2. "Neanderthal." *Encyclopaedia Britannica*. Encyclopaedia Britannica, 2013. Web. 5 June 2013.

3. "El Castillo: Earliest Known Cave Paintings Might Have Been Made by Neanderthals." *HuffPost: Arts & Culture*. HuffingtonPost.com, 16 May 2013. Web. 5 June 2013.

4. Jean Clottes. "Chauvet Cave: France's Magical Ice Age Art." *National Geographic*. National Geographic Society, 2001. Web. 5 June 2012.

5. Ibid.

6. "Cueva de las Manos, Río Pinturas." *UNESCO*. United Nations, 2013. Web. 9 Sept. 2013.

7. "Accidental Archaeological Discoveries: Photos." *Discovery News*. Discovery Communications, 12 Dec. 2012. Web. 9 Sept. 2013.

8. Michael Ray Taylor. *Caves: Exploring Hidden Realms*. Washington, DC: National Geographic, 2000. Print. 85.

9. Mark Jenkins. "Deep Southern Caves." *National Geographic*. National Geographic Society, June 2009. Web. 18 June 2013.

10. "Big Room Self-Guided Tour." *Carlsbad Caverns*. National Park Service, n.d. Web. 17 June 2013.

11. "Carlsbad." *Weekend Explorer*. PBS, n.d. Web. 9 Sept. 2013.

12. James M. Tabor. *Blind Descent: The Quest to Discover the Deepest Place on Earth*. New York: Random, 2010. Print. 171.

13. "Western Caucasus." *UNESCO*. United Nations, 2013. Web. 9 Sept. 2013.

14. James M. Tabor. *Blind Descent: The Quest to Discover the Deepest Place on Earth*. New York: Random, 2010. Print. 159.

15. "National Speleological Society." *National Speleological Society* National Speleological Society, n.d. Web. 17 June 2013.

CHAPTER 4. EVOLVING EQUIPMENT AND TECHNIQUES

1. James M. Tabor. *Blind Descent: The Quest to Discover the Deepest Place on Earth*. New York: Random, 2010. Print. 21.

2. Ibid. 161.

3. Ibid. 32.

4. Ibid. 173.

5. Ibid. 174.

6. Ibid. 159.

7. Ibid.

8. Ibid.

9. Ibid. 160.

CHAPTER 5. DATA, DYES, AND DISCOVERIES

1 William Stone and Barbara am Ende with Monte Paulsen. *Beyond the Deep: The Deadly Descent into the World's Most Treacherous Cave*. New York: Warner, 2002. Print. 311.

2. Ibid. 317.

3. James M. Tabor. *Blind Descent: The Quest to Discover the Deepest Place on Earth*. New York: Random, 2010. Print. 173.

4. Ibid. 168.

5. Ibid. 14–15.

6. Ibid. 21.

7. Ibid. 24.

8. Ibid. 9.

9. Ibid. 159.

10. Ibid. 160.

11. Ibid. 59.

12. Ibid. 60.

CHAPTER 6. CAVE DIVING AND CAMPING

1. William Stone and Barbara am Ende with Monte Paulsen. *Beyond the Deep: The Deadly Descent into the World's Most Treacherous Cave*. New York: Warner, 2002. Print. 144.

2. James M. Tabor. *Blind Descent: The Quest to Discover the Deepest Place on Earth*. New York: Random, 2010. Print. 44–45.

3. Ibld. 47.

4. Ibid. 41.

5. Ibid. 41–42.

6. Michael Ray Taylor. *Caves: Exploring Hidden Realms*. Washington, DC: National Geographic, 2000. Print. 110.

SOURCE NOTES CONTINUED

7. William Stone and Barbara am Ende with Monte Paulsen. *Beyond the Deep: The Deadly Descent into the World's Most Treacherous Cave*. New York: Warner, 2002. Print. 227.

8. Michael Ray Taylor. *Caves: Exploring Hidden Realms*. Washington, DC: National Geographic, 2000. Print. 80.

9. James M. Tabor. *Blind Descent: The Quest to Discover the Deepest Place on Earth*. New York: Random, 2010. Print. 120.

CHAPTER 7. EXTREME ENVIRONMENTS

1. Garry K. Smith. "Eisriesenwelt - Ice Cave." *Newcastle & Hunter Valley Speleological Society*. Newcastle & Hunter Valley Speleological Society, June 2012. Web. 9 Sept. 2013.

CHAPTER 8. SCALING HEIGHTS, DIVING DEEPER

1. "Grand Canyon." *Encyclopaedia Britannica*. Encyclopaedia Britannica, 2013. Web. 5 June 2013.

2. Michael Ray Taylor. *Caves: Exploring Hidden Realms*. Washington, DC: National Geographic, 2000. Print. 155.

3. "Geologic Formations." *Carlsbad Caverns*. National Park Service, 19 Aug. 2013. Web. 9 Sept. 2013.

4. James M. Tabor. *Blind Descent: The Quest to Discover the Deepest Place on Earth*. New York: Random, 2010. Print. 180-182.

5. Ibid. 183.

6. Miki Meek. "Racing to the Center of the Earth." *National Geographic*. National Geographic Society, Feb. 2004. Web. 9 Sept. 2013.

CHAPTER 9. UNDERGROUND ADVENTURES TODAY

1. James M. Tabor. *Blind Descent: The Quest to Discover the Deepest Place on Earth*. New York: Random, 2010. Print. 246.

2. Ibid. 245.

3. Ibid. 249.

4. Mark Jenkins. "Vietnam Cave." *National Geographic*. National Geographic Society, Jan. 2011. Web 19 June 2013.

5. "Krubera Cave: The First 2000m+ Cave on Earth." *Speleogenesis*. Speleogenesis, n.d. Web. 9 Sept. 2013.

6. Michael Ray Taylor. *Caves: Exploring Hidden Realms*. Washington, DC: National Geographic, 2000. Print. 147.

7. Neal Shea. "Cavern of Crystal Giants." *National Geographic*. National Geographic Society, Nov. 2008. Web. 9 Sept. 2013.

8. Ibid.

9. Ibid.

10. Michael Ray Taylor. *Caves: Exploring Hidden Realms*. Washington, DC: National Geographic, 2000. Print. 187.

11. Miki Meek. "Racing to the Center of the Earth." *National Geographic*. National Geographic Society, Feb. 2004. Web. 9 Sept. 2013.

INDEX

ABOUT THE AUTHOR

Rebecca Felix is a writer and editor from Minnesota. She has a bachelor of arts degree in English from the University of Minnesota Twin Cities, and she has worked on numerous publishing projects for children and young adults. Topics Rebecca has written about or worked on editorially include energy alternatives and conservation, genetics, social change, and civil rights.